# THE POWER OF GOD
# AND THE
# gods OF POWER

# THE POWER OF GOD
# AND THE
# gods OF POWER

## Daniel L. Migliore

**Westminster John Knox Press**
LOUISVILLE • LONDON

© 2008 Daniel L. Migliore

*Book design by Sharon Adams*
*Cover design by designpointinc.com*

*First edition*
Published by Westminster John Knox Press
Louisville, Kentucky

This book is printed on acid-free paper that meets the American National Standards Institute Z39.48 standard. ∞

PRINTED IN THE UNITED STATES OF AMERICA

08 09 10 11 12 13 14 15 16 17 — 10 9 8 7 6 5 4 3 2 1

**Library of Congress Cataloging-in-Publication Data**

Migliore, Daniel L.
    The power of God and the gods of power / Daniel L. Migliore.
        p. cm.
    Includes bibliographical references.
    ISBN 978-0-664-23164-4 (alk. paper)
    1. Providence and government of God—Christianity.   2. Power (Christian theology)   I. Title.
BT96.3.M54 2008
231.7—dc22

                                                2007031896

*To Luca and Matteo*

# Contents

# Preface

$T$he present volume is a thorough revision and enlargement of my little book *The Power of God* published by Westminster Press in 1983.

I accepted the invitation to have another try at this topic for two reasons. First, because I believe all theological reflection is provisional and unfinished. The story is told that when asked whether he was a revisionist theologian, Langdon Gilkey, an influential theologian of the twentieth century, is reported to have quipped, "Yes, I must be, because whenever I read something I have written, I say to myself, 'That has to be revised!'" Like all theological topics, our understandings of the power of God must be open to revision again and again in the light of the biblical witness. Thinking of God neither as sheer power on the one hand nor as simply powerless on the other can be an option if our reflection is rooted in that witness.

Dramatic changes in our world in the past quarter century provide a second reason for my taking up the topic of the power of God anew. While the understanding of the power of God and its relationship to the powers of the world is a perennial issue of Christian faith and theology, theology is always done in particular contexts. In the early 1980s the Cold War was still being waged, though it would soon be officially ended with the fall of the Berlin Wall and the collapse of the Soviet Union. Hope for a more peaceful world, however, was rather quickly dashed. Instead, after 9/11, and with the growth of Islamist militancy, the launching of counterterrorist wars, and the tactic of suicide bombings that kill and maim innocent civilians, the world has become an even more dangerous place than it was in 1983. The question of power—its use and abuse—and especially the sanctioning of violence in the name of God is an inescapable theological and political issue of our generation. I have tried to expand and update the thesis of the book with these present realities in mind.

Yet with all the changes that have occurred on the international scene and in theological discussion, two things about this book remain unchanged from my earlier effort. The first is the central thesis that the gospel of Jesus Christ crucified and risen for the salvation of the world challenges us to a thorough rethinking of what we understand to be the power of God and the way in which human power might be exercised as a faithful witness to God's power. A second point of continuity between this volume and its predecessor is the primary readership to which it is addressed. Now as before I have tried to offer a clear, readable, and provocative book for beginners in theology rather than for professional theologians. My aim has been to show what is distinctive about the power of God according to the biblical witness, and how this understanding of God's power profoundly affects how we live and how we exercise power both as individuals and as communities and nations.

I am grateful to the editors of Westminster John Knox Press, especially to Donald McKim for encouraging me to write this volume, and to Daniel Braden and Gary Lee for their editorial expertise. Hearty thanks also go to my good friends John and Maureen Stewart, who read the entire manuscript and whose comments helped make it more accessible to budding theologians in seminaries and in local congregations than it otherwise would have been. The faults that remain are, of course, my own. Finally, my thanks to the Trustees and Administration of Princeton Theological Seminary for the sabbatical leave during which this book was written, and above all, thanks to my wife, Margaret, for her strong support in the undertaking and for her careful proofreading of the galleys.

1

# The Question of God's Power

*Who is God except the LORD?*
(Ps. 18:31)

## Our Experience of Power and Powerlessness

People ask about the power of God for many reasons. Some ask out of awe at the immensity and beauty of the cosmos. Others ask out of doubt and skepticism. Still others ask out of anger, fear, or desperation in their experience of the absence of God. While for a few the question of the power of God may be an intellectual game, most people ask about God and God's power because the question is of overriding importance in their lives.

A woman lies awake in her hospital room in the middle of the night. She knows she has an incurable cancer. During the last few weeks, she has had a lot of time to think—about herself, about her family, about her work, about the meaning of life. She is frightened, as never before, by her sense of helplessness. Until recently, she had always been in control of her life, a person who took charge of things. Not only her family but many other people depended on her apparently endless vitality and strength. Not an especially religious person, she now raises questions that she never considered very important before. In the stillness of her hospital room she wonders: "God, do you really care for me? Can I count on you to help me in the difficult days ahead?"

In an inner-city church a young black pastor sits at his desk and ponders what he will say to his congregation on Sunday morning. Most of his people are unemployed. Their hope for a new and better life is vanishing. They are weary of fighting city hall about their wretched housing conditions and the pathetic resources and standards of the schools in their community. Whenever the pastor looks at his congregation from his pulpit, he sees etched in their faces their many years of suffering and helplessness. Locked in a situation where the future seems to offer only more of the same, the pastor is moved to question God. "Do you really care for these poor and oppressed people? Don't you see that their lack of power to make a difference is robbing them of all hope? Are you really with us and can you really help us?"

A judge sits alone in her chambers. She must sentence a teenager who has been convicted of a serious crime. While he has shown remorse and does not have a record of other offenses, the district attorney's office, the editors of the local newspapers, and many people in the community want the judge to issue the toughest sentence possible. They want it to be a stern message that will deter other criminal acts by young people in their town. Contemplating her options, the judge silently prays, "My duty is to uphold the law. Does respect for the law leave any room for mercy? Will you help me to render a judgment in this case that is both just and wise?"

Whether sick or healthy, male or female, black, brown, or white, most of us can recognize something universally human in the questions of these three people. Like the dying woman and the struggling black pastor, at some point we all come up against forces beyond our control. When that happens, we know what being powerless means. While few of us have a position of authority and responsibility equal to that of the judge who must sentence a convicted youth, all of us, simply in our day-to-day decisions, exercise some measure of power and have to take responsibility for the choices we make.

It is in our experiences of power and powerlessness that the question of God arises. Even if unspoken or neglected for long periods of time, this question never entirely dies out. That is because it is not a purely academic but a profoundly practical question. It arises not at the periphery but at the very center of human life.

When people ask about God and God's power, they seldom want to know whether God's existence can be proved. Many philosophers and theologians, of course, like to ask that sort of question. They endlessly debate proofs for or against the existence of God. Such debates, however, are far removed from the concrete life experiences of power and powerlessness that move people to ask about God.

The question of God is not limited to a particular type of experience or to a single sphere of human existence. It may be asked when we marvel at the beauty of life, or when we grieve at the loss of life. It may arise at the birth of a child, or at the death of a child. It may take the form of a cry of thanksgiving for the goodness of life, or of a cry that comes, as the psalmist says, "out of the depths" (Ps. 130:1).

We may ask about God when we undertake perilous tasks with uncertain outcomes. We may ask about God when we have to make decisions that will seriously impact the lives of others. We may ask about God because we have become acutely aware of our own vulnerability or the vulnerability of a loved one, and we seek a life-giving power beyond our own resources. We may ask about God because our life seems broken or empty, and we look for a source of renewal and transformation. We may ask about God because we are burdened with guilt from which we find no relief, and we seek a word of forgiveness powerful enough to heal us. We may ask about God as we struggle against overwhelming forces of bondage, injustice, and hatred. The question of God and God's power is raised in these and countless other situations in which we experience both the possibilities and the limitations of our own power in a world of multiple and sometimes hostile powers.

Experiences of both power and weakness, and along with them the question of God, are woven into the fabric of life. Every human being, indeed every living creature, possesses and exercises power to some degree. We exercise power in everything we do, even in the smallest step we take. To be human is to have some power, to be able to do something, to reach a goal, to make a difference in the world. There is no life where there is no power. Possession and exercise of power is a necessity of life.

At the same time, to be human is also to experience the limits of our power, to become aware of our dependence on persons and powers beyond ourselves. No one is absolutely independent. No one is completely autonomous. As we act, we discover that we are not alone;

we are surrounded by others who also exercise power. What these others do affects us, and we need their help and support. No one can successfully navigate the turbulent waters of life entirely on her own. This partial but necessary dependence on others is no more inherently evil than is our power to act and to make a difference. Human beings are social beings. All of us live in a network of relationships with others that sometimes augments our own strength and sometimes exposes our dependency. When the powers that surround us overwhelm us, we experience powerlessness.

Multiple, interacting, and often conflicting powers are at work in every sphere of human life. The powers in and around us are marked by ambiguity. This is true in our development as persons with particular abilities and strengths, in our existence in the world of vast social and political powers, and in our dealings with the forces of nature.[1]

Consider first the sphere of personal development. An infant cries in order to get her mother's attention. While this is a very small display of human strength, if the infant were unable to call for attention, she might be neglected and quite possibly die. A teenager wants some independence from his parents. If he offered no resistance at all to his parents' ideas and expectations, his growth toward maturity and adulthood would be blocked. In every stage of human life, the capacity to exercise some power is needed.

Our development as persons takes place in relationships with others. According to the Bible, human beings are created in and for relationships. "Male and female he created them" (Gen. 1:27). To be in relationship is to act and be acted upon. We are both agents and patients, both actors and sufferers of power. We cannot become mature, responsible persons without some confidence in our own powers. Equally true, however, is that we cannot become mature, whole human beings without a basic trust in powers beyond our own. According to developmental psychologists, a fundamental trust by the infant in the surrounding world, and especially in the mother, is an essential element in human growth. From infancy to old age we are interdependent beings. Human relationships are thus a delicate interplay of power exercised and power suffered. Sometimes we experience cooperation, partnership, and a sharing of power with others. Other times we feel harmed and made helpless by the actions of others. When we are honest, we recognize that we too have sometimes used our own power in ways that have harmed others and may even have rendered them helpless. The experience of power in our personal development and our everyday relationships is marked often by ambiguity and sometimes by abuse. The abuse of power is a prominent manifestation of what the Bible calls sin or acting contrary to the will of God for human life.

Another sphere in which the complex interplay of power and powerlessness is encountered is our social, economic, and political life. Indeed, the realities of power and powerlessness are experienced most acutely in the world of impersonal constellations and networks of power. Vast amounts of power and influence are embodied in a host of public realities—governments, corporations, schools, science and technology, the arts, the mass media, cultures, social movements. These great powers compete and often clash with one another as each seeks to extend its influence. One corporation vies to get the advantage on its competitor. A dominant culture may try to control, eliminate, or absorb a minority culture. The precarious "balance of power" among nations is shattered when one nation seeks to acquire economic or military domination over neighboring nations. As in our personal relationships, power and powerlessness are inescapable realities of the social and political worlds that we all inhabit. In fact, the term "power" is most frequently used in this sociological and political meaning of the ability of one group or class or nation or civilization to compete with others and, where possible, to gain control over others.

The Bible is very much aware of the reality of vast impersonal power networks in which human life is lived. It calls these constellations of power the "principalities and powers" of this world. Traditionally, these powers have been understood as supernatural beings like angels and demons, but they can also be viewed as powerful forces and structures of our common human life—nations, institutions, systems of law and order, forms of culture. They are the "rulers," "authorities," "powers," of this world (Rom. 8:38–39; Eph. 3:10; 6:12). Although part of God's creation, they are always ambiguous in their bearing on human life. They are established to serve God's purposes and can do much good. But they can also be turned to destructive ends. Think of modern science. It has clearly brought enormous benefits to humanity. Yet we also know that science can be turned against human welfare. When the first atom bomb was exploded in the desert of New Mexico, Robert Oppenheimer, one of the leaders of the project, quoted the Bhagavad Gita: "Now, I have become Death, the destroyer of the world."

Or think of the ambiguity of the power of nations and empires. The apostle Paul exhorts Christians to respect the authority of the state. "There is no authority except from God," he says (Rom. 13:1). As a Roman citizen, Paul knew the benefits that were provided by the Roman Empire: maintenance of social order, freedom to speak in public, a system of roads that made travel and communication over large distances possible, the right of judicial appeal. But like other "rulers and authorities" of the world, nations and empires are often far from benign. They frequently make extravagant demands, abuse their power, and employ it to evil ends. The systematic abuse of power is a potential threat in every social and political order. Sin and evil are not restricted to personal relationships; they are also at work in the institutions of government, in science, and in economic systems. If Paul can encourage Christians to respect civil authorities as instituted by God, the writer of the book of Revelation can describe the Roman Empire as a devouring dragon (Rev. 13). Walter Wink sums up the New Testament understanding of the ambiguity of these powerful institutions and structures of the world: "The powers are good; the powers are fallen; the powers must be redeemed."[2]

Experiences of power and powerlessness occur in still a third sphere: our dealings with our natural environment. Here again we encounter both ambiguity and abuse. Through science and technology human beings have acquired the ability to control many forces of nature and to use them for the achievement of human aims. When given absolutely free reign, however, human exercise of power over nature can be destructive rather than beneficial. Technologically advanced societies not only use but abuse the natural environment. Our polluted air, water, and fields, and the dangerous warming of the earth as a result of unchecked use of carbon fuels are evidence of human misuse of power over nature. Such misuse of power damages the delicate ecological balance that makes life on our planet possible. Ironically, in our reckless conquest of nature, we increasingly experience the limits of our capacity to undo the harm we have inflicted.

While modern science and technology have given humanity remarkable control over nature, we know that this power too is far from absolute. Human beings often find themselves helpless before the awesome manifestations of the power of nature in events like hurricanes, earthquakes, floods, drought, and disease. Hurricane Katrina devastated New Orleans in August 2005. A huge tsunami in the Indian Ocean killed some 230,000 people in December 2004. These are vivid reminders of how powerful the forces of nature can be and how small the powers of humanity seem by comparison. In our relationships with nature, as in our personal relationships and in our existence in a world of vast impersonal networks of social and political forces, human beings are made aware that they are both agents and sufferers of power.

What I have said so far has aimed at making two basic points. The first is that being human has very much to do with the experience of power and powerlessness, with the use and abuse of power. As Bishop Stephen Sykes puts it, we find ourselves in "a world of overlapping and intersecting powers in which we are enmeshed."[3] We need to possess and exercise some power; yet our power is limited, and we need to be able to trust in the helpful exercise of power by others. Power is necessary to act, to grow, to create, to help shape our own lives and the world around us. At the same time, when power is used to enlarge the self at the expense of others, when it is exercised oppressively rather than cooperatively, it brings ruin and misery to all dimensions of life. As already noted, the arrogant assertion and misuse of power is a symptom of what the Bible calls sin. Human sin, and the misuse of power that accompanies it, takes both personal and institutional forms, and it has consequences for the whole of creation.

Not surprisingly, many people today are cynical about every form of power. They echo the famous statement of Lord Acton: "Power tends to corrupt, and absolute power corrupts absolutely." There is much truth in this statement, and it is dangerous to deny it. But it is not the whole truth. Power in the form of unrestrained self-assertion and the will to dominate others is certainly evil. What Acton's statement fails to acknowledge, however, is that if power tends to corrupt, the condition of powerlessness is also destructive of full human life. Our humanity is corrupted when we abuse power; our humanity is diminished when we are rendered powerless.

The second point of these initial reflections is that the question of God and God's power—when it is not a merely academic question—is raised in the midst of the concrete realities of life where power is both used and profoundly abused. We may ask about the power of God in those moments when we are conscious of possessing great power, or at those times when we have been stripped of all power. We may look to God's power when we yearn to be released from a weight of guilt that threatens to paralyze us and rob life of all joy, or when we experience the gradual or sudden loss of our power because of illness or old age. We may question God's power when we encounter the tremendous power of "the principalities and powers" of this world, when we see the poor trampled on, or innocent people tortured or murdered by ruthless regimes. We may take offense at God's power if it does not protect us from the forces of nature that may strike us suddenly and with cata-strophic results. We may despair of God's power when we realize how vulnerable our natural environment is to human exploitation and abuse.

The urgency of the question of God and God's power is ignored in ivory tower debates about the existence of God, or in cocktail party chatter about the latest church scandal or the latest theological fad. The question of God is alive, however, in the midst of real-life expe-riences in which people have to make momentous decisions, or con-front the abuse of power, or face the abysmal misery of powerlessness. Is there a power that works unambiguously for the flourishing of life? Is there a power that does not crush human beings but empowers them and enters into creative partnership with them? Is there a power that does not oppress but sets people free? Is there a power that does not deceive but can be trusted in life and in death? Is there a different form of power, a "power of God for salvation" (Rom. 1:16)? Is the ultimate power at work in this world of countless and conflicting powers friendly or hostile, gracious or malevolent, concerned or indifferent to our longing for new and transformed life? These are the real ques-tions people ask when they ask about God and the power of God.

## Faith in God as Reliance on the Ultimate Power

If the question of God and God's power arises in the context of our everyday experiences of power and powerlessness, in its deepest form the question of God is the question of the nature of ultimate power. What power is finally sovereign in our world, and how is it to be described?

The close association of power and God is a universal religious phenomenon. In all religions God is experienced as awesome power, power that evokes wonder and fear. God is mysterious power that both attracts and frightens us. The power of God is described as superior to all other powers because it has the capacity to create and to destroy. From the dawn of human history God has been the name of overwhelming power. The sages of ancient Greece taught that "all things are full of gods." Each of the gods of ancient Greek religion was connected with a life power experienced as irresistible or overwhelming: Aphrodite, the power of sexual attraction and fecundity; Dionysius, the power of wine and ecstatic joy; Athena, the power of wisdom; Apollo, the power of the arts; Ares, the power of war; Zeus, the power of destiny.

Although today we no longer give personal names to the many powers that surround us, they are factors of life and compete for our allegiance. They compel us to ask which power we will acknowledge, not just in theory but in everyday practice, as ultimate. Faith in God involves a fundamental decision about the ultimate power at work in the world. As theologian Paul Tillich explains, our "ultimate concern" is what we recognize as having the power to threaten and to save our very being.[4]

Recent opinion polls continue to show that a very large majority of American adults confess a belief in God or in a universal spirit. On the surface such statistics are impressive. But the question whether God exists misses the real issue of faith. The far more telling questions are: Who or what is the God in whom we trust? What do we believe God is really like? What difference does belief in God make in our everyday lives?

A view of faith in God is superficial if we imagine that it involves no more than saying yes to the question: Does God exist? Real faith in God goes much deeper. To believe in God is to trust in the power that has created and rules the world. It is confidence in the power that governs our lives and guides the course of history. It is reliance on the power worthy to judge us and able to save us from our bondage to the power of sin and death. It is commitment to the power that rightfully claims our worship and unconditional allegiance.

Whatever we look to as the ultimate power capable of giving our lives meaning and fulfillment is our God. Martin Luther expresses this point with great clarity. In an incisive passage of his *Large Catechism* he writes: "A God is that to which we look for all good and where we resort for help in every time of need. To have a God is simply to trust and believe in one with our whole heart. . . . The confidence and faith of the heart alone make both God and an idol. . . . Whatever your heart clings to and confides in, that is really your God."[5]

Luther's classic statement of what it means to believe in God makes several important points. First, it declares that faith in God involves passionate trust rather than mere intellectual curiosity or casual assent to traditional beliefs. Faith in God is never partial; it involves the whole person. In faith we entrust ourselves to God unconditionally, or as Luther says, with "our whole heart." The passionate act of faith is far from intellectual sport; faith means clinging to God in life and in death.

Second, for Luther a God is someone or something to which one looks for saving power, for wholeness and meaning in life, for "all good," for "help in every time of need." To have a God is to affirm that the power we call God is able to bring us to fulfillment. A God for Luther is, therefore, not just the ultimate power but the ultimate good. Luther's own religious quest went far beyond simply asking, Does a God exist? or, Is there an ultimate power? His burning question was: How can I find a gracious, a benevolent, a saving God?

Third, Luther's statement implies that we may in fact have a "god" even when we do not recognize this to be the case. On the theoretical level, we may ignore or deny the reality of God. But in actual life practice, we demonstrate otherwise. However enlightened, agnostic, or even atheistic we may be in relation to traditional beliefs about God, we nevertheless have something that functions in our life as a god. We recognize in practice one of the powers within us or outside us as our ultimate good. We all have, in Tillich's words, our "ultimate concern." We all give our heart to something, allow something to become our highest value, our highest priority in life. We may not consciously acknowledge that we have a god in this sense, but the fact is evident from our practical decisions and our way of life.

In one of her short stories, Flannery O'Connor describes a social worker named Sheppard. He is an enlightened man who thinks that talk of demonic power and the need for the redeeming power of Jesus is rubbish. Sheppard is totally dedicated to rescuing the under-privileged; it is, we might say, his religion, his ultimate concern. He is convinced that he is able, through his own powers of intelligence, understanding, and patience, to bring about the moral transformation of a clever but mean and hardened boy named Rufus. Consumed by his passion to change Rufus, Sheppard systematically neglects and often cruelly berates his own son, who is only an average ten-year-old and certainly far less intelligent than Rufus. In the end, Sheppard awakes to the fact that he has not only failed miserably in his effort to "save" Rufus; he also discovers, too late, that he has deprived his own son of the love that he wanted and needed.[6]

Some of the ultimate concerns to which people wholeheartedly give themselves are noble and admirable. These would certainly include causes like universal human rights and "liberty and justice for all." Other ultimate concerns are mean and shoddy, such as the reckless pursuit of wealth, success, or endless sexual adventures. Still other ultimate concerns are obviously demonic, such as militaristic nation-alism, or the claim to racial superiority.

Whether we acknowledge it or not, we all recognize some cause, some principle, some power as ultimate in our life. Consciously or not, we entrust ourselves to this power perceived and valued as being of surpassing worth. In our hearts we confess, "Thou art my God." Of course, we may flit from one "god" to another. As long as we are estranged from the true God revealed in Jesus Christ, we are likely to have many gods and to rely on them for help in our helplessness.

## Faith in God versus Faith in the gods

Luther's statement lights up still another feature of faith in God—the necessity of distinguishing between the true God and idols. Only the Lord God is worthy to be the object of our total and unconditional love and loyalty. The true God is radically different from the gods to whom we are tempted again and again to give our heart. We may and do have many commitments; we may and do recognize the importance of many causes. If we have faith in God, however, we will refuse to allow any of these other concerns to become what is ultimately important in our life.

The God of the biblical witness is a "jealous" God. The first of the Ten Commandments declares emphatically: "You shall have no other gods before me" (Exod. 20:3). God wants our complete and undivided trust and allegiance. When Jesus is asked what is the greatest of the commandments, he replies: "You shall love the Lord your God with all your heart, and with all your soul, and with all your mind" (Matt. 22:37). If we rightly understand and obey this commandment, we will also understand and obey its inseparable companion: "You shall love your neighbor as yourself" (v. 39).

Love for one's family is a fine thing. But when it substitutes for love of God and love of all God's children, it becomes an idol. Patriotism—the affection and loyalty one has for one's native land—is surely a noble sentiment. But when patriotism challenges or even replaces one's love for and loyalty to God and God's righteousness, it turns into an idol.

An idol is anything we substitute for the true God. We expect our idols to fill our lives with meaning, to make us happy, to supply us with whatever we need. We look to the idols to protect us from our doubts about our worth, from our feelings of guilt and emptiness, from our fears of weakness, suffering, and death. But the idols cannot deliver what they promise and what we expect of them. Entrusting ourselves to idols leads not to fulfillment but to self-destruction and quite frequently to the destruction of others as well. Every idol is like the sorcerer in the legend of the sorcerer's apprentice. The power given to us by the idol quickly overpowers us and makes us its slave.

The idols of power are within us and around us. They compete for our allegiance. Knowledge is power, we are told. Money is power, others say. Power comes from the barrel of a gun, according to the vigilante or the revolutionary. These are only a few of the more common confessions of where ultimate power is sought and found in our time. The true God also exercises power. As the apostle Paul writes, "The kingdom of God depends not on talk but on power" (1 Cor. 4:20). But the power of the kingdom of God is altogether different from the power of the idols. Christ is "the power of God" (1:24), and his different power is exercised in his servant ministry and finally in his cross and resurrection. According to Paul, the power of God is at work in the "weakness" of the cross (v. 23). The gospel of the crucified Lord is, paradoxically, "the power of God for salvation" (Rom. 1:16). When one entrusts oneself to the true God whose strange power is manifest even in the weakness of the cross, one is inevitably thrust into the struggle between God and the gods. When faith in the God of the gospel dawns in human life, all our supposedly powerful gods lose their control over us.

In the late nineteenth century, the philosopher Friedrich Nietzsche spoke through a prophet he named Zarathustra to announce the "death of God." During the late 1960s and early 1970s this theme was picked up by several American theologians and attracted national attention. Its premise was that modern people no longer had any interest in or need of God. They were now fully mature and could manage quite well without the God hypothesis. The movement did not survive long. It was influenced too much by the optimistic spirit of the time. It judged that modern science and technology made faith in God meaningless. This was a serious miscalculation. Today we are acutely aware that modernity and its use of power is thoroughly ambiguous; it is both bane and blessing. Even if those who occupy positions of power cease asking the question of God, those who live on the underside of history, those who suffer the consequences of the abuses of power, will continue to ask the question.

Nevertheless, as a diagnosis of our social and cultural attitudes, we must recognize a measure of truth in the talk of the "death of God." It exposed what we all too often acknowledge as the power able to threaten and save us. We are inclined to see real power in the Pentagon and the Kremlin, in nuclear weapons and laser beams, in the huge oil and pharmaceutical companies, in space technology and gross national product, in the mass media and the superstars of popular culture. What can the power of the kingdom of God embodied in a crucified Christ mean in comparison with these very real and awesome powers that profoundly impact our lives from cradle to grave?

If old gods die, new gods are born. Despite its secularism, our age is far from godless. Religion is booming in America today, and some of it is frankly idolatrous. Often our piety takes the form of polytheism—the worship of many gods. Finite powers and limited causes are elevated to divinity. The consumption of material goods and reliance on nuclear armaments are high in the pantheon of gods that promise us fulfillment or safety and claim our total allegiance. Advertisements ask us to believe that if we have new cars, bigger homes, better clothes, and all sorts of electronic gadgetry, we will find happiness. At the level of national policy, we are encouraged to trust in ever more powerful machines of war and highly sophisticated missile defense systems as the guarantee of our personal and national safety.

In view of the many gods that inhabit our world, we do well to recognize that the word "God" is much more ambiguous than is commonly thought. It has many different and even contradictory meanings. "God" is a word used to express both love and hate. It is a word of blessing and a word of cursing. In the name of God a Mother Teresa tends the sick; in the name of God a suicide bomber kills himself and many innocent civilians. The word "God" seems to be able to underwrite both generous lives and savage crusades.

This is why faith in God—the living God of the Bible—must be distinguished continually from faith in the gods. When faithful to its Lord, the community called the Christian church does not confess its faith in God in vague, abstract terms. It bears witness to the God of the Bible who speaks and acts in particular ways. When God is known supremely in the person and work of Jesus Christ, in his ministry, cross, and resurrection, all our gods become no-gods. They are exposed as gods of our own making. Faith in God necessarily includes struggle against the gods. It subverts commitment to other gods, and demotes them from the status of divinities to that of finite powers placed under human responsibility.

We cannot think or speak properly of God, as the Bible uses this word, without taking part in this conflict between faith in God and allegiance to the many idols of our making. A choice must be made. As Elijah warned the people of Israel on Mount Carmel, it is impossible to go limping forever back and forth between God and the gods (1 Kings 18:20–21). Just as plainly, Jesus said: "No one can serve two masters; for a slave will either hate the one and love the other, or be devoted to the one and despise the other. You cannot serve God and wealth" (Matt. 6:24). The power of God is totally different from the power of the idols, and we are confronted with the choice as to which power we shall worship and serve. For Jesus and the prophets of the Old Testament, the choice is clear. The prophets mock the gods made by human hands. They deride the lifeless idols that cannot speak, act, or even move, and have to be carried around by their makers (Isa. 46:5–7). Repeatedly, the prophets summon the people to decide whether they will worship the living God or give themselves to idols whose promise of saving power is empty.

All our questions about God, and most especially about the power of God, are like boomerangs. They have a way of turning back upon us and changing into the questions: Who is the God whom *you* will trust and serve? What power do *you* acknowledge as divine and worthy of your worship? What power will *you* allow to claim your whole being—your mind, will, and affection—in an age when power is exercised destructively by many and suffered grievously by many others?

As I shall try to show in the following chapters, the power of the living God of the Bible is radically different. It is different from the power exercised by our many personal and corporate idols. Even if the Christian church in its proclamation and practice has not always honored the difference, it remains no less real. The living God is not a projection of our will to power or our deep-seated desire to dominate others. While majestically strong, the living God shows that strength most awesomely in the humility of a servant Lord. The living God is not the guarantor of the way things are but the disturbing God who keeps us restless for a transformed world. Creator and redeemer, the living God is full of surprises and repeatedly challenges all our presuppositions about what it means to be truly divine and what it means to be truly human. Altogether different from the dead idols that we fabricate with our hands or construct in our imaginations, the living God is strong enough to will to be with and for his creatures, to become vulnerable for their salvation, and to triumph in his vulnerability. The living God exercises power even in weakness and exposes the weakness of our vaunted powers. Christians are called to love and obey the living God who exercises power so differently. They are called to take part in this power of God by loving their neighbors, including their neighbors called enemies.

As the prophets of ancient Israel declared and as Jesus of Nazareth proclaimed and demonstrated, the power of God is different. We need to know the difference between the power of the living God and the distorted images of divine power that haunt our lives. A critical look at the images of God's power abroad in American culture and society today is the task to which we now turn.

## Questions for Discussion

1. What experiences of power and/or powerlessness in your own life have been occasions for wondering about the power of God?
2. How do you understand the claim that everyone has some sort of "god"? Do we all look to someone or something to give meaning to our life and to provide us with hope?
3. Jesus commanded us to love God with all our heart, soul, mind, and strength, and to love our neighbor as ourselves. Can you think of ways obedience to these commandments would require us to struggle against all other gods?

2

# Images of God's Power
in American Culture

*You shall have no other gods before me*
(Exod. 20:3)

## Knowledge of God and Knowledge of Ourselves

At the very beginning of the *Institutes of the Christian Religion*, John Calvin tells his readers that knowledge of God and knowledge of ourselves are inseparable. Each significantly influences the other. On the one hand, if we begin with self-knowledge, we discover how weak and needy we are, and we are led immediately to consider how great and majestic God is. On the other hand, if we begin with recognition of the beauty and holiness of God, we soon have to acknowledge our own unhappiness and sinfulness. Knowledge of God and knowledge of ourselves are so intertwined that Calvin thinks it is difficult to say with which we should begin.[1]

Calvin's point is clear enough. We can, however, add a corollary to his insight about the connection of knowledge of God and knowledge of ourselves: A distorted understanding of God will be accompanied by a distorted understanding of ourselves, and a flawed understanding of ourselves will be accompanied by a flawed understanding of God. This is the version of Calvin's principle that I want to explore in this chapter.

In one of his short stories, Sherwood Anderson gives a vivid portrayal of the way distorted images of self and distorted images of God interlock. It is the story of Jesse Bentley, a pious, prosperous, and hardworking farmer. Jesse comes from a long line of strong men. He wants his farm to produce more than any other farm in the state. Above all, he wants to be the father of sons who will be rulers, just as the biblical Jesse was.

Jesse believes in an austere and powerful God who controls human destiny even if he remains deeply hidden. In Jesse's mind, he is following God's will by working hard to acquire possessions, by exercising dominion over the earth, by ruling over the members of his family and others dependent on him, and by siring male children who will be rulers in their turn.

As he grows older and more prosperous, Jesse is no longer content with his six hundred acres. He covets his neighbor's property as well. Convinced he is God's chosen, Jesse looks upon his neighbors as Philistines, enemies of God. He fears that a Goliath will come from these Philistines to take away his land and possessions. So Jesse prays for a son whom he will call David. Eventually a grandson by that name comes under his charge. One day the grandfather accompanies the young boy into the forest. The boy wants to go hunting with his slingshot, but Jesse secretly plans to sacrifice a lamb and dedicate his grandson to God. Frightened by his grandfather's strange behavior, David runs away. When Jesse pursues him, the terrified boy picks up a stone, places it in his slingshot and hurls it at the old man. Jesse is stunned and rendered helpless; the boy is never seen again.

Anderson's story shows how our distorted understandings of God's power are intertwined with our exaggerated understandings of our own power. Jesse's God is a reflection of himself. He wills to dominate others. In his lust for power, Jesse fears the coming of a Goliath to rob him of his land. Yet Jesse himself has become an oppressive Goliath whose destructive dream of power is finally ended by the slingshot of a frightened young boy. Jesse's hunger for power costs him his beloved grandson. His understanding of power, divine and human, is his undoing. As in the biblical story, the true power of God proves to be at work not in strong Goliath but in weak David.[2]

If knowledge of God and knowledge of ourselves are as intertwined and as subject to distortion as both Calvin the theologian and Anderson the short-story writer say, how do we break out of the vicious cycle? How do we achieve a proper knowledge of God and a proper knowledge of ourselves?

The answer is that we do not achieve this on our own. If the cycle of distorted knowledge of God and distorted knowledge of ourselves is to be broken, we must receive wisdom from beyond ourselves. A gift must be given. A light must shine. In the language of Christian theology, that light and that gift are called revelation, what God does to disclose himself and his will. Reliable knowledge of God must be based not on our own ideas of who or what God is but on God's self-revelation. Christians turn to the Bible as the primary witness to this revelation. What they find there are not just historical facts and religious poetry but witness to God's gracious covenant with the people of Israel that culminates in God's personal presence and activity in Jesus Christ for the reconciliation and redemption of the world. This witness of the Bible to God's self-revelation in Christ is regulative for the faith and life of the church.

But aren't the biblical writers human as we are? Aren't they also limited and fallible? Don't they also bear witness to God in ordinary human language? When they speak of God, don't they also make use of words, images, and metaphors that are drawn from human experience and that are ordinarily used to describe the objects of our everyday world? Yes, to all these questions. Nevertheless, Christians hold that these biblical witnesses, in all their humanity, are used by God to point to God's own self-revelation. The biblical witnesses themselves are not the revelation; they are the primary witnesses to the revelation. They are servants of the revelation who are used by the Spirit of God to point to the light of God that shines above all in the face of Jesus Christ. Christians must therefore be guided and continually corrected by the biblical witness in their thinking and speaking of God.

If the biblical images of God, as well as our images of God dependent on the biblical witness, are fully human, does this mean that there is no true, reliable knowledge of God? No, but it does mean that our language about God is never exhaustive, never beyond the need of correction and deeper understanding. No image of God that we employ is directly identical with the reality of God. Our words can point to but cannot fully capture the reality of the living God. That said, it makes a great difference which images and metaphors guide the way we think and speak about God. If Christian faith is not simply believing *that* God exists but believing *who God is* and *what God is like*, then the particular images and metaphors we use are crucial. In faith and theology, as in all our knowledge, the limits of our language are the limits of what we are able to see. Images and metaphors can help us see things that we did not see before. As theologian Colin Gunton put it, "metaphor can have a revelatory function."[3]

When the biblical writers bear witness to God, they speak with a wealth of images and metaphors. Some of these are taken from the world of nature—God is like a rock (Ps. 28:1), a light (Ps. 27:1), a fire (Exod. 3:2). Other images come from the sphere of personal relationships—God is like a mother (Isa. 49:14–15), a father (Matt. 7:11), a husband (Hos. 2:16), a friend (Jer. 3:4). Still others come from the world of work—God is like a shepherd (Ps. 23:1), a potter (Rom. 9:21), a builder of a city (Heb. 11:10). And still others come from the political sphere—God is like a king (1 Sam. 12:12), a lord (Rev. 17:14), a judge (Isa. 33:22). Even from this brief summary, it is clear that all language about God, including the language of the Bible, involves the exercise of human imagination. In our language about God, images, similes, and metaphors abound. The parables of Jesus often begin: "The kingdom of God is like. . . ."

While cherishing the great diversity of biblical images of God, the Christian community has always placed special emphasis on speaking of God as personal. This emphasis has sometimes been criticized as "anthropomorphism," which means thinking and speaking as if God resembled a human being. Some philosophers and theologians would prefer to call God the "Supreme Being," or "Being-Itself," or the "First Cause," or the "Highest Good." But such language seems cold and abstract to most believers. In any case, the authors of the Bible show little hesitation in speaking of God with the help of "anthropomorphic" images. They are not embarrassed to speak of the strong "arm" of God, or the "eye" of God, or of God's having compassion on the poor, or of God's being angered by injustice.

In spite of the suspicion that surrounds anthropomorphic language about God, speaking of God in personal terms has always commended itself as both necessary and appropriate to Christians of every age for two basic reasons. The most important reason is the conviction that in Jesus of Nazareth God has freely and graciously entered into human life as one of us. In the ministry, death, and resurrection of this Jesus,

God has revealed who God is and what God is really like. According to the biblical witness, Jesus is the Word of God become flesh (John 1:14). He is Emmanuel, God with us (Matt. 1:23). He is God's only Son given for our salvation (John 3:16). He is the perfect "image of the invisible God" (Col. 1:15). In the "face of Jesus Christ" we see the glory of God (2 Cor. 4:6). In Jesus, God speaks to us not just in words but in the person and work of his very own Son (Heb. 1:1–2).

The second reason Christians deem speaking of God in personal terms appropriate is the conviction that human beings have been created in the "image of God" (Gen. 1:27). Being in God's image does not mean that human beings bear a physical resemblance to God. Nor is its meaning to be found primarily in the fact that humans are free, rational creatures and thus bear the marks of the living God who knows and wills. Most profoundly, to say that human beings are created in the image of God is to say that we are made for life in communion with God and one another. Even as God loves us and enters into relationship with us, so human beings reflect or "image" God when they love God and neighbor. Because we are sinners, our true humanity in the image of God has been defaced, and we see its true contours only in the new humanity of Jesus Christ.

Let's return now to Calvin's principle of the connection of knowledge of God and knowledge of ourselves. If we speak of Jesus Christ as *the* image of God, and speak of ourselves as created in this image, we are saying that all understandings, all images of God and of ourselves are to be measured finally by Jesus. Serious problems arise when we turn this procedure around and begin to think and speak of God as made in *our* image. It is one thing to confess Jesus Christ as the revelation and action of God in human form. It is something entirely different to think and speak of God and Jesus as merely symbols and reflections of whatever we hold to be good and worthwhile in human life.

Thinking and speaking of God as one who addresses us in the biblical witness to Christ locates the source of our knowledge of God outside ourselves. Thinking and speaking of God as our highest ideal or as an expression of what we most desire or fear makes what we call God an extension of ourselves. But the living God is not a bigger and stronger version of who we are. God's love is not our love writ large.

God's power is not the magnification of whatever power enlarges us. This way of thinking of God leads to idolatry. We end up imagining God in a way that suits our own wants and interests. We project ourselves onto a reality that we call God, but what we call God is only our mirror image. We talk of God, but we are really talking about ourselves. The human imagination is extraordinarily skilled in making God look, think, and act just like us. In our captivity to sin, our imagination works like "a perpetual factory of idols," as Calvin puts it.[4] We think of God as a mirror image of our sinful selves: God confirms our ideals, endorses our values, and defends our way of life.

Calvin's critique of the human tendency to manufacture gods after our own image should disturb us. It exposes a secret that we would rather keep hidden. All knowledge of God, like other kinds of knowledge, is colored by our personal interests or those of the group to which we belong. We usually have no difficulty seeing this process at work in other people. We readily note how their way of thinking of God seems comfortably tailored to their own benefit. More difficult to detect, however, are the ways in which our own thinking and acting, in matters of religion or otherwise, are influenced by our own economic and social interests or those of our own community. If we are beneficiaries of the present social order, we are likely to uphold it and resist any significant changes. However, if we experience deprivation or severe disadvantage in the present social order, we are likely to have a strong interest in promoting changes that will improve our lot and that of others in our condition. These conflicting human interests will affect our thinking and speaking about God. Moses believed that God wanted the Hebrew slaves in Egypt to go free. Pharaoh clearly thought otherwise. Our knowledge of God—and in particular our understanding of divine power—is often influenced by our special interests, whether personal, economic, or political. Theology that fails to take this fact into account is neither serious nor honest. To paraphrase Calvin, our self-centered, class-centered, and nation-centered interests are a perpetual source of idols.

All this suggests that the workings of religion in human life are ambiguous and sometimes deceptive. As Calvin and Anderson in their different ways alert us, knowledge of God and knowledge of ourselves move back and forth. What results from this movement depends greatly on what the source of our knowledge is. Our understanding of God may be shaped by what we consider valuable and desirable, and we may try to model ourselves after whatever we imagine God to be like. We develop our humanity according to the image of the God who rules our life. If our God is a warrior bent on conquest, we will gladly march off to annihilate our enemies. If our God is a merciless judge of all who transgress the established law, we will be similarly severe in our judgment of all transgressors.

Faith in the living God is a humanizing force; faith in idols that caters only to our self-interests or the interests of our clan or nation is a terribly destructive force. While there can be no knowledge of God apart from our act of reception, it is not God who is to be conformed to us but we who are to be conformed to God's self-revelation in Jesus Christ as attested in Scripture and illumined by the power of the Holy Spirit. We must be liberated from our sinful bondage to ways of thinking and speaking of God that are determined by our personal interests or the dictates of our group or culture. This liberation comes from the self-revelation of the living God whose ways are not our ways (Isa. 55:8), and whose exercise of power differs so radically from the power of the gods who rule our lives.

## Images of God's Power in American Popular Culture

Christian faith must approach every human culture with a critical eye. It will say yes to what is true and good in a culture, and no to what is false and demeaning. A blanket endorsement of any culture would be a failure of Christian witness. This holds for both high culture and popular culture.

Popular culture is a window through which we can discover some of the ways a society imagines God to be like as well as what it most admires and fears of human beings. Even when the images of divine and human power in popular culture are not made fully explicit or do not become the subject of reflection, they often lurk beneath the surface of everyday life. American popular culture confirms Calvin's contention that there is a reciprocal relationship between our images of God and our self-images. On occasion, ways of thinking of the power of God and human power found in American culture may dimly reflect traditional Christian teachings; more often, they stand in sharp contrast to those teachings. Let's look at three ways the power of God is expressed, sometimes in a serious vein and sometimes with humor and parody, in popular culture in America.

1. One way of picturing Godlike power in American culture is *sheer almightiness.* We could demonstrate this by an examination of attitudes expressed and language used in extolling the power of our computers, high-powered automobiles, champion sports teams, the invigorating life provided by new prescription drugs, and other familiar phenomena of American society. I will focus instead on the representation of power inscribed with great clarity in the American myth of the superhero.

Versions of this myth find relatively innocent expression in tall tales of a figure like Paul Bunyan. Far more violent forms of the myth are found in films of the old West, and more recently, in the crusading adventures of the superheroes of comic books, video games, and films. The superhero has many names: Superman, Superwoman, Batman, Captain America, Spiderman, Rambo, Hulk, and countless others. All of these superheroes are mighty defenders of justice, law, and order. Their wide appeal rests on their superhuman power that enables them to conquer forces of evil in the world. The world is out of joint, and someone must set it right. In their righteous crusades, the superheroes do not hesitate to use violence against violence. Violence in the cause of righteousness is unavoidable, and the superheroes employ it without compunction to redeem a world in peril.

The superheroes are agents of redemptive violence. In their study of the myth of the American superhero, John Shelton Lawrence and Robert Jewett conclude that this myth "secularizes the Judaeo-Christian dramas" and reflects "a hope for divine, redemptive powers that science has never eradicated from the popular mind."[5]

A prayer of Homer Simpson from one of the episodes of the popular television series *The Simpsons* discloses the often merely implicit connection between the figure of the superhero and the saving power of God. Finding himself as usual in a serious predicament, Homer prays: "I'm not much of a praying man, but if you're up there, please save me, Superman."[6]

If we ask what image of God's power the myth of the superhero reflects, the answer is clear: the power of God is almightiness. God is the almighty warrior, the almighty vindicator, the almighty guardian. God's power is pure omnipotence. True divinity is known by its capacity to deliver a knockout blow to every opposition. If we are moved to worship such a God, it is not primarily because of the divine goodness or beneficence but because the power that this God wields gets the job done with dispatch and by whatever means necessary. The American superhero is a miniature replica of the almighty God who is able to blow away all opposition. The superhero/God is our ideal self made after the image of what we assume the omnipotence of God to be like, the redeemer "who has dropped the ineffectual baggage of the Sermon on the Mount."[7]

Ironically, while the link between the adventures of the superhero and the power of God seems strong in American popular culture, the appeal of almighty power quickly diminishes when it takes concrete form in an employer, or a government official, or a religious leader. The philosopher Charles Hartshorne suggests that some people may have a boss at work who rules his employees just as a dictator rules the inhabitants of his realm. They may be inclined to think of God as the world boss whose iron hand controls everything. In the presence of an employer who must have everything just his way, or before a God seen as world boss, no questions are to be asked. One simply does what one is told. According to Hartshorne, this view of divine omnipotence is simply "a theological mistake."[8]

Some contemporary theologians contend that the idea of divine power as sheer almightiness is enshrined in the traditional image of God as "father." God is the great patriarch, lording it over the lesser members of the family or tribe. God the father, it is charged, is the archetype of the domineering male who demands that others submit unconditionally to his will. God as father, the charge continues, is the chief buttress of sexist oppression. More than that, this patriarchal image is the religious support for the image of authoritarian power in all spheres of life—in education, church, business, and politics. In all these areas, the "fathers" possess and exercise unchecked and often abusive power.

No doubt both church and society have given reasons for these charges. Speaking of God as father has too often been misunderstood and abused. For some women and men alike—especially those who have experienced abuse in childhood—it has become an image to be rebelled against rather than the symbol of a caring and gracious God.

What this criticism of the image of God as father may overlook, however, is the radical revision of the understanding of the fatherhood of God found in the New Testament. A familiar example is Jesus' parable of the Prodigal Son whose father readily forgives his wayward child and joyously celebrates his return home. This parable portrays God as father in a way that is far removed from the understanding of father as a tyrannical or abusive figure. Equally important is the New Testament depiction of Jesus' own relationship to the one he calls "Abba" or "Father." The father of Jesus is merciful (Luke 6:36), gives good gifts to his children far beyond the gifts that earthly fathers give to their children (Matt. 7:11), and is completely trustworthy in life and in death (Luke 23:46). The New Testament's designation of God as father bursts wide open our common understandings and uses of the term.

That said, the picture of God's power as almightiness, whether as divine warrior, supreme monarch, world boss, or domineering father, still reigns in many quarters today. Belief in God is thereby set in irreconcilable conflict with all the movements of enlightenment and emancipation that have characterized modern society at its best. Distorted by the image of sheer almightiness, God becomes the symbol of repression and resistance to change. It is not surprising, then, that for some people today reflection on God's power has taken the form of a critical question. Is the ultimate power of this world identical with the power of control and compulsion familiar to some from their own personal and social histories and associated in their minds with the figures of the feared tyrant or the authoritarian father?

If the church continues to employ the image of God as father (which it should), the image must be purified of its patriarchal connotations and interpreted in the light of the gospel of Jesus Christ. If the church continues to speak of Jesus as Lord (which it should), the image of lordship must be clearly distinguished from dictatorship and bossism and transformed by the story of the servant lordship of Jesus. A perennial task of the church is to engage in careful and critical reflection on all of its words and images of God. The church's witness must always be more than a mere echo of the voices of the surrounding culture.

2. A very different conception of the power of God in American popular culture is that of a *captive power*, a power who is useful to us and is at our beck and call. God is like Santa Claus. He comes on schedule and gives us what we want. In one *Peanuts* comic strip, Lucy insists that Santa Claus does not owe Linus anything. To which Linus replies, "He does if I've been good! That's the agreement!"[9]

Like its apparent opposite—the image of God as sheer almightiness—the view of God's power as our captive takes many forms. In one form, God is understood as a kind of business partner. If we do something for God, God will do something for us. We are related to God in an exchange process; there is a trade-off between God and us. This picture of God is based on a system of merit. We are repaid for our good deeds or for our proper ritual performances. The repayment may come in the form of happiness and success in the present; or it may be postponed to another life after death. In any case, God is imagined as having entered into a contractual relationship with humanity that is based essentially on the principle of business exchange or of receiving what one is due. Such an understanding of our relationship with God happens to correspond with the underlying principles of our economic and social systems.

The captive God also appears under the guise of a magician who is asked to pull all sorts of rabbits out of the hat for our benefit. If you want a promotion at work, or a new car, or a winning ticket in the lottery, just ask the great magician and you will receive your wish. Mark Twain had his finger on this understanding of God in American culture in his description of an incident in *Huckleberry Finn*. Wanting to instill some religion in Huck, Miss Watson tells him that if he prayed every day he would get whatever he asked for. Huck tries out the suggestion, and prays for some fishhooks. When after several tries he does not get the fishhooks he has prayed for, he gives up the practice of prayer as useless. "There ain't nothing in it," he concludes.[10]

At the heart of every image of the captive God is the idea that God is not so different from us and that we can cajole or persuade God to give us what we want. The captive God is like a dog on a leash. God does not govern *us*; *we* control God. The assumption here is that all power can be manipulated if one is clever enough, and God happens to be that power which, if properly approached, can get us whatever we want, especially if we are in a jam. The practice of trying to control God is very old. It is the essence of religion as magic. According to religion as magic, divine power can be harnessed by the proper ritual or the right words to bring about a desired effect. While we may dismiss this view of God as a feature of archaic religions, there are numerous ways in which religious people today try to use God for their own interests.

Infamous forms of faith manipulation are found in fictional figures like Elmer Gantry—a successful con artist in the form of a revivalist preacher. But there are more than a few real-life figures who persuade their followers that God can be used, and who fill their own pockets in the process. The idea that God is "useful" to help us achieve success and prosperity is more widespread than we may be willing to admit. The gospel of prosperity is a small cottage industry in America. If only you believe hard enough, or live a decent life, you will be duly rewarded. The use of God is evident not only in Elmer Gantry-like ministries and in many business enterprises, but also in the political arena. When the name of God is invoked to provide a religious halo to a burst of nationalism, or a political campaign, or a new business venture, God is being "used." God is used by the politician or the political party that drums up financial support by peppering its advertisements with religious-sounding slogans. God is used by the television preacher who promises healing for an infirmity if the viewer will only say a little prayer and send in a cash contribution.

In these and countless other ways, God is taken captive by us. God is compelled to serve our personal wishes or our social and economic interests or projects. Our captive God is given our allegiance if he gives us what we want, if we are guaranteed happiness now or in the hereafter, if we are assured that God is on our side and upholds the values we espouse. Such a God is useful to us in establishing and maintaining what we consider to be the good, happy, and successful life. The captive God is our supreme genie, our personal or national champion who blesses us and does our bidding.

The modern criticism of religion draws much of its strength from these closely related images of God as business partner, magician, and champion—all views of God as a captive, serviceable deity, who responds to our infantile demands and who sometimes enters into an unholy alliance with misery and injustice. The images of God as captive power are examples of the kind of "bad faith" that is severely criticized by Marxists and other militant atheists, and their criticism surely contains a measure of truth.

The critique of the captive God, however, has a source far deeper and stronger than the modern despisers of religion. When the prophets of Israel excoriated the people of God for substituting religious ritual for doing works of justice and mercy, they were exposing and condemning attempts to use God rather than to serve God. All three stories of the temptations of Jesus emphasize his rejection of any effort to use God. God is not to be used for one's personal benefit (turning stones into bread, Matt. 4:2–4), or for some sensational demonstration (jumping from the pinnacle of the temple, vv. 5–7), or for the acquisition of power over others (ruling over all the kingdoms of the world and controlling all their power and wealth, vv. 8–10). The Old Testament prophets and Jesus proclaimed the living God who is altogether different from the little gods manufactured by our fears and desires. The living God shatters our distorted images of divinity and stands in judgment on every effort to manipulate divine power and grace.

3. A third image of God's power in popular culture is one of *ineptness or indifference*. The inept God is the butt of Woody Allen's remark that in view of the condition of the world, God is an underachiever. Somewhat less blunt but not dissimilar in its message is the film *Bruce Almighty*. When Bruce thinks things are not going as they should, God challenges him to take over the rule of the world and see if he can do a better job. Endowed with the powers of deity, Bruce discovers that the task turns out to be more than he can handle. Implied in the plot and in the depiction of God in the film is the idea that God is doing the best he can with an impossible job.

If one wants to avoid thinking of God as inept, an alternative is to imagine God as simply indifferent. According to this image of deity, God exists in splendid isolation from the world. God is apathetic. God is not affected by the weal or woe of creatures. After creating the world, God is now safely removed from what happens in it. God is the "absolute," and absolute means totally unrelated to anything else.

The power of God is here imagined as above and outside the sphere of our existence, unconnected with worldly events and human history. God is entirely free from the suffering and misery of the world. God is uninvolved and unconcerned.

This is an image of God with a long history. Aristotle spoke of God as the "Unmoved Mover," the supreme being who moves the world by the power of attraction but remains entirely unmoved and unaffected by what happens in the world. Eternity is untouched by time. God is alone in splendid perfection, neither wanting nor needing anything. God has no friends, said Aristotle. To have a friend is to cherish another and to allow oneself to be affected by another, and a true God can have none of that. The ancient Stoics also imagined the supreme reality as indifferent and apathetic and tried to adopt that serene, detached attitude as much as possible in their own lives. Through apathy one becomes invulnerable to the affliction of this world. If one is perfectly apathetic, one never need suffer grief. Grief is the experience of loss. An indifferent, apathetic God never suffers loss, never laments, never weeps. An indifferent God never rejoices in the presence of another because that too would invariably result in painful loss should the source of delight go away or die.

In the eighteenth century a modified version of this image of God as perfectly indifferent appeared in a form called deism. According to the deists, God is too great and too exalted to be intimately involved with the day-to-day affairs of the world. Like an expert clockmaker, God has made the world and allows it to run completely on its own. Clockmakers who have to repair their clocks only display their lack of mastery of their craft. God is the perfect clockmaker whose supreme ability is expressed in the world process, which never needs divine assistance. The God of deism is an armchair deity.

The picture of God as indifferent and aloof, like the other images of God we have considered, is no more than a projection of our own wishes and fears. We project onto God our own ideal of the strong individual who is supposedly totally independent of others. Many popular self-help philosophies, which talk much about self-realization, rest on this ideal of human selfhood. Individuals possess all necessary value and power within themselves. One may enter into occasional negotiations with others, but such relationships are temporary arrangements and not really essential. The image of an absolute, indifferent God goes hand in hand with the picture of the ideal individual human being as a completely autonomous self. The wisdom of the indifferent self and the apathetic God is: "Don't invest yourself in the lives of others. Don't commit yourself very deeply to any relationship. You may get hurt. Play it cool."

The image of the indifferent God and the corresponding ideal of the solitary, independent self are socially and spiritually bankrupt. Today we are increasingly aware of the interdependence of all life. The idea of an absolutely independent, completely self-made individual is an empty, destructive myth. If it is an error to idealize the utterly self-sufficient human being, it is equally mistaken and equally destructive to think and speak of God as indifferent and aloof. The image of God as indifferent may strike some as philosophically sophisticated, but it holds little comfort for people whose lives are crushed by unrelieved suffering or unforgiven guilt. The murder of millions of Jews in Nazi Germany, the destruction of countless people in Stalin's concentration camps, the massacres in Rwanda and Darfur would mean nothing to the Unmoved Mover. The loss of a child in a tragic automobile accident would have no effect on an indifferent God. The affliction suffered by a cancer patient would meet with no response from a God who is defined as absolute and apathetic.

This is not to deny that terrible experiences of the absence and silence of God may be part of the life of faith. Job experienced this terrible absence, and he voiced his lament and protest. Jesus experienced the absence of God when he cried out on the cross: "My God, my God, why have you forsaken me?" (Mark 15:34). But the experience of the absence and silence of God, known in a unique way by Jesus and in a lesser way by countless human beings, is something entirely different from a view of God as uninterested and unrelated to us. The passionate cry of Jesus on the cross is a cry to God whose nearness Jesus knew and proclaimed throughout his ministry. Jesus does not cry into the cosmic void as one abandoned by an apathetic deity. He wants to experience God's nearness again and trusts that this will happen: "Father, into your hands I commend my spirit" (Luke 23:46).

The more we look to the New Testament Gospels, the clearer it becomes that the image of the isolated, indifferent god is an idol that reflects our own idea of the perfectly unattached and independent self. It has nothing to do with faith in the living, compassionate God who for us and for our salvation humbled himself, lived among us as a Servant-Lord, rejoiced at the marriage in Cana, fed the hungry, healed the sick, wept at the tomb of Lazarus, sweat blood in the Garden of Gethsemane, and died as a criminal on a cross.

## The Partial Truth of Atheism

The images of the tyrannical God, the captive God, and the indifferent God are grotesque distortions of the Christian understanding of the ultimate power we call God. What is at stake in these distortions is not simply a mistaken doctrine of God. As noted at the beginning of this chapter, our images of God and our understandings of self and society influence each other. The dangers posed by false images of God are not only theoretical but also practical. Where there is distortion in our understanding of God, there is also distortion in our understanding and practice of human life. When we misconceive divine power, we will almost certainly misconceive and misuse human power.

The image of the all-powerful, domineering God breeds inordinate pride and self-righteousness. In the image of this God, we may see ourselves as God's superheroes employing whatever means necessary to counter evil and protect the good. If God's rule over us takes the form of unlimited control over impotent subjects, then the master-slave relationship in human society finds justification in religious belief. The only way finally to be free from coercive powers symbolized by the almightiness of divinity and practiced by earthly tyrants is to repudiate their authority and topple their thrones.

The image of the captive God breeds complacency, self-deception, and exploitation. If God can be bought off, if God can be used to satisfy our every whim and desire, why should we not also use our fellow creatures in this way? Moreover, if the captive God is on our side, we must always be in the right, and whatever we do to further our cause will have God's blessing. The captive God is unable to exercise judgment on us and unable to act in new and unexpected ways. Our self-interests and our established way of life become the measure of all things, including God.

The image of the indifferent God breeds hopelessness and resignation. If God is aloof and unaffected by what happens in the world, then the beauty and tragedy, the joy and affliction, the gross injustices and noble sacrifices of human history, have no real and lasting significance. What happens in time is, as Shakespeare's Macbeth rues, "a tale told by an idiot, full of sound and fury, signifying nothing." Depression and despair seem the only option for suffering and oppressed men and women if the ultimate power that rules the universe is unaffected by their cries.

Thus Christian faith in God acknowledges the partial truth of atheistic critiques of religion. All of our understandings and images of God must undergo a testing of the most radical sort. They must be tested by the revelation of God that culminates in the person and work of Jesus Christ. As we have seen, even beloved biblical images of God, such as "Father" and "Lord," are not immune to this process of critical testing. While our understanding of God may begin with familiar and unexamined images such as "'Father," through the process of testing we gradually become aware that the Bible radically redefines the meaning of this title. When Jesus calls God "Father," he does not mean the authoritarian and oppressive father figure so familiar to many people from history or from personal experience. In his teaching and self-giving life and death, Jesus redefines what it means to call God "Father." Only when we have permitted the symbol of father to go through the fire of critical testing and have retrieved its fundamental biblical meaning are we able to use it again freely and gladly. When this happens, we also make the joyous discovery that the Bible can speak of God as mother as well as father (even if God's fatherhood and motherhood far transcends our experience of fathers and mothers). Similarly, when Jesus is called "Lord," the meaning of this title will not be defined by the actions of the Caesars of this world, but by the life, ministry, death, and resurrection of Jesus.

Jürgen Moltmann, a prominent contemporary theologian, makes a highly provocative remark about the partial truth of atheism. In response to Ernst Bloch, a neo-Marxist philosopher who wrote, "Only an atheist can be a good Christian," Moltmann replied, "Only a Christian can be a good atheist."[11] These are extremely paradoxical statements. They require careful interpretation, for on the surface they simply appear nonsensical.

The first half of the paradox—"Only an atheist can be a good Christian"—is a rhetorical way of saying that only if we are prepared to expose the idols at work in our own life and in human affairs generally can we call ourselves Christians. Faith in God necessarily struggles against faith in the gods. There is no genuine faith without this struggle. There is no faith in the true God without our disbelieving in—saying a mighty no to—the gods who reflect our own narrow personal wishes and the exclusively self-serving policies of our nation or society. In this sense there is a long tradition of "atheism" in Christianity. In fact, during the first few centuries of the church, Christians were charged with atheism because they refused to acknowledge and worship the gods of the Roman state. To put it bluntly, when the early Christians confessed that Jesus is Lord, they were also declaring, Caesar isn't.[12]

A Christian need not be afraid of the critique of the gods by unbelievers. Indeed, some of their criticism may be true, and we disregard it at our peril. It can serve to purify authentic faith in God. To pretend that beliefs about God do not sometimes function as infantile dreams of omnipotence (Freud), or as a kind of drug that anesthetizes people to the wretchedness and suffering of life (Marx), or as a camouflage of our resentment and desire for revenge (Nietzsche), or as an excuse for rejecting the findings of modern science (Dawkins), is to stick our head in the sand.[13] False images of God are real forces in human life, and they are dehumanizing. Faith in the living God puts to flight all of these false gods of our making. There is, therefore, a place for "atheism" in Christian faith and life. Not in the sense that we deny the reality of the living God but in the sense that we happily bid goodbye to all false and dehumanizing idols. Christians will also be ready to recognize that the reason some people refuse to believe in God is that they cannot accept the many distorted ideas of God with which they are familiar, not because they necessarily reject the reality of God revealed in Jesus Christ.

The second half of Moltmann's paradox is equally startling: "Only a Christian can be a good atheist." Here the claim is made that only faith in the living God is able to protect and promote what the atheist holds to be of great value—our true humanity. Many atheists deny God for the sake of humanity. That is, they deny God for a world free of injustice and oppression in which all men and women can hold their head high. The Christian has no quarrel with the denial of the God the atheist denies: the God whose existence deprives humanity of life and freedom. The God of Christian faith, however, is not the enemy but the friend of true human freedom. When atheists in their justified repudiation of the idols also reject the God made known in Jesus Christ, they open the door to the rule of human life by new idols. In their zeal to cast out the demons that ruin the house of humanity, they overlook the crowd of new demons who enter in unobserved (cf. Luke 11:24–26). After the disclosure of the horrors of the labor camps and the systematic repression of dissidents in officially atheistic societies, it is no longer possible to argue convincingly that atheism automatically brings increased concern for human freedom and welfare and the unimpeded pursuit of truth.

Our life becomes truly human when faith in God is boldly and continuously distinguished from faith in the gods of our own making— the gods of brute force, self-centeredness, and indifference. Paul Lehmann, an influential American theologian of the twentieth century, gathered in a single phrase the practical significance of faith in God. According to Lehmann, God's work in the world is that of "making and keeping human life human."[14] We might add to Lehmann's phrase that we can become responsible participants in God's work in the world only if we "recognize and keep on recognizing that God is God." Human life becomes and remains human when it is lived in trust and confidence in the God whose power is unlike all other powers. The power of this God is the power of self-giving, liberating, renewing, and reconciling love.

In every age, faith in God must contend with the gods that populate our imagination and that control our personal lives, our social institutions, and our cultural creations. The God of the biblical witness is entirely different, as I will try to show in the following chapter.

## Questions for Discussion

1. How would you explain the difference between saying we are created in God's image and thinking of God as made in our image?

2. Can you think of novels, movies, or paintings in which God is pictured in ways that correspond to what is described in this chapter as "the tyrant God," "the captive God," and the "indifferent God"?

3. What sense can you make of the provocative statements: "Only an atheist can be a good Christian; only a Christian can be a good atheist"?

# The Biblical Witness to God's Power

*I am among you as one who serves*
(Luke 22:27)

## Different Ways of Reading and Misreading the Bible

Like every religious text, the Bible can be read in many different ways. There are no red-letter instructions at the beginning of the Bible saying, "Read this text in this and only in this way...."
Even a cursory review of some of the ways people inside and outside the church read the Bible today confirms the variety of interpretive possibilities that it offers.

In a highly influential study of the history of biblical interpretation, theologian Hans Frei traces "the eclipse of biblical narrative."[1] According to Frei, two ways of interpreting the Bible in the modern period have replaced the church's earlier reading of the Bible as an overarching story or drama of God's dealings with the world.

One modern approach to biblical interpretation searches for the historical facts behind the text. This approach is best known in the form of the "quest of the historical Jesus." Here the primary question is not, How do the Gospels describe Jesus? but, What can we know for certain about the real Jesus on the basis of modern historical science? This way of approaching the Bible has made important contributions to our knowledge of the history of ancient Israel as well as to our understanding of the context of the ministry of Jesus and the diversity of the earliest

Christian communities. The resulting pictures of Jesus, however, are strikingly divergent and sometimes contradictory.

Another modern way of reading the Bible, according to Frei, is to harvest its universal moral teachings. We may not be able to agree on the nature of God or the divinity of Jesus, but there are universally valid moral principles embedded in the biblical texts. The Golden Rule, "Do to others as you would have them do to you," is one such universal moral principle found in the Bible. In both the historical-critical and the moral approaches to biblical interpretation, the Bible's own narrative description of the identity and purposes of God often drops from view. The Bible no longer describes the real world in which God is active and into which readers are to be drawn. Instead, readers of the Bible take from it what they deem valuable, or what can fit into their own prior knowledge of reality.

We can add to Frei's analysis three other ways of reading the Bible today that minimize or ignore its overarching drama. One is to read the Bible as a textbook in science. The first chapter of Genesis, which describes God's creation of the world in six days, is viewed as a literal, scientific account of the beginnings of the universe and of life on earth. This reading of the biblical story of creation runs contrary, of course, to modern physics and cosmology that speak of the billions of years the universe has existed as well as to modern evolutionary science that describes the changes that have occurred over time within and among species. Those who insist that the Genesis story of creation is a scientific account of the origin of the world seem to assume that the majesty and power of God would be diminished if the Bible were not read as providing us with accurate scientific descriptions of how long the creation of our universe has taken and by what process life has developed on our planet.

Another way of reading the Bible today that has a wide following is to approach it as a book of prophecy. If literalist interpretations of the Genesis account concentrate on the beginning of the world, those who read the Bible as a source of prophecy focus on when and how the world will come to an end. This way of reading the Bible highlights the book of Revelation. It finds there detailed and accurate predictions of events soon to occur that will bring all history to a close. Since the 1970s this way of interpreting the Bible has been promoted by books like Hal Lindsey's *The Late Great Planet Earth* and the even more influential Left Behind series by Tim LaHaye and Jerry Jenkins.[2] These writings are supposedly based on the predictions of the end of the world contained in the Bible. Recent conflicts in the Middle East and the continuing threat of terrorist attacks and nuclear war seem to confirm for many people the validity of looking to the Bible to provide a description of the countdown to the end of the world. If a literalist reading of the creation stories in Genesis assumes that the power of God is vindicated only if the universe took its present form within the span of a week or at most in a few thousand years, the doomsday reading seems to assume that God will be shown to be truly powerful only if the world goes up in flames within our lifetime.

Still another way of reading—or more accurately, misreading—the Bible is to use it as a springboard for sensational novels and movies that purport to disclose some secret about the life of Jesus. One example is Dan Brown's popular novel, *The Da Vinci Code*.[3] As a work of fiction, one might concede that Brown's book has some entertainment value. As such, it is harmless enough. The problem arises when readers, including church members, become so enamored with the plot of Brown's story that they virtually allow it to displace interest in the story of Jesus as recounted in the Gospels. Brown's novel turns on an assumed intimate relationship between Jesus and Mary Magdalene that resulted in the birth of a child. According to the novel, knowledge of these facts has been suppressed by the church, and the secret, known only to a few, was locked in coded form in Leonardo da Vinci's famous painting of the Last Supper. Brown's book is typical of sensational takeoffs from the Gospels that can become major distractions from the Gospels' own accounts of God's redemptive activity in the ministry, passion, and resurrection of Jesus.

If the readings of the Bible I have briefly summarized tend to constrict and distort its witness, what constitutes a good and responsible reading of the Bible? I suggest it would be a reading that attends closely to the particularity of the biblical witness. It would be a reading that lets the Bible tell in its own way the story of God's dealings with the people of Israel and God's presence in Jesus Christ for the reconciliation of the world.

All of the world religions speak of God within a particular faith tradition. This is certainly true of Judaism, Christianity, and Islam. While the understandings of God in these faith traditions have significant similarities, each speaks of God in distinctive ways. They all rely on particular scriptures, tell particular stories of decisive revelations of God, and emphasize the importance of participation in the life and worship of a particular community of faith in which these stories are told and retold. The Christian understanding of God rests on the special revelation of God's activity to which the Old and New Testaments bear witness.

Christians look to the Bible as the unequaled source of illumination of who God is, what God has done, what God has promised, and what God summons us to be and do. Throughout the history of the church, the biblical witness has shaped Christian faith and practice. This is not to say that Christians reverence the Bible as a book that has fallen down from heaven. Nor is it to say that the significance of the Bible resides in some theory of its supernatural origin or in a doctrine of its complete inerrancy. Reading the Bible as if it were an encyclopedia of revealed truths leads to serious misunderstandings of God and God's purposes. The Bible has a central story; it is more like an epic drama than an encyclopedia.

As Christians read the Bible, its authority rests not in itself but in the one to whom it bears witness. The Bible witnesses to God's surprising and costly love for the world embodied in the person, ministry, crucifixion, and resurrection of Jesus Christ. With Jesus at its center, the drama of the biblical witness, illumined by the Holy Spirit, plays an indispensable and normative role in the life of the Christian community. As we hear and take to heart the biblical stories, teachings, prayers, warnings, and promises, and as we pray for the guidance of God's Spirit, we begin to see God and ourselves in a new light. We begin to see the world as it truly is and as God intends it to be. "What is in the Bible?" asks the theologian Karl Barth. History? Morality? Religion? Yes, all these things. But in and beyond them, says Barth, there is a "strange new world within the Bible."[4] If we attend closely to the biblical witness, we find ourselves in the new world of God, who turns upside down all our understandings of who God is, what God purposes, and what power God exercises. We could easily imagine a Christian community without church buildings, or robed choirs, or ordained clergy. But we cannot easily imagine a Christian community that does not listen again and again to the witness of the Bible, and above all to its witness to Jesus Christ as God with us and for us. Christian faith in God is awakened, reformed, and nourished again and again by the biblical witness to Christ.

Thus without denying that God may be known in some fashion apart from the revelation attested in Scripture, Christians find the key to knowledge of God, whatever its source, in the scriptural story of the crucified and risen Jesus. He is the definitive revelation of God, the unique embodiment of the very life and power of God. Our understandings of God and ourselves are judged and transformed by his life, ministry, death, and resurrection.

As the "power of God for salvation" (Rom. 1:16), the gospel or "good news" of Jesus draws all of our ideas and images of God into a continual process of correction and transformation. We are never finished with learning and relearning what it means to understand God in the light of the gospel of Jesus Christ rather than on the basis of the idols that we construct and that so often rule our lives.

This means that all of our images and names of God, however cherished, have to take on new and different meanings from what they previously had. When we speak of the "love," or "wrath," or "freedom" of God, the meaning of these words is not to be determined finally by the way they are understood on the basis of our personal experience, or on the meaning they might have in contemporary culture. The "love" of God as defined in the gospel story is far more than affection. The "wrath" of God cannot simply be equated with what we experience as anger. The "freedom" of God is very different from doing whatever one pleases.

So it is with the biblical understanding of the power of God. A rethinking of the meaning of power is called for. If we attend closely to its story, the Bible subverts and transforms our conventional understandings of power. As Copernicus started a revolution in astronomy by declaring that the earth rotates around the sun rather than the sun around the earth, so Christians participate in a revolution in the understanding of God's power. They find the central clue to the meaning of the true power of God not in their own ideas, nor in the views of what constitutes power current in their culture, but in who Jesus is and what Jesus does, according to the witness of Scripture. Christians are called to live on the basis of this new understanding.

## The Exodus Power of God

From beginning to end, the Bible proclaims the sovereign and gracious power of God. The Bible opens with the majestic declaration: "In the beginning God created the heavens and the earth" (Gen. 1:1). It ends with jubilant affirmations of the coming manifestation of the triumph of God at the conclusion of history: "Hallelujah! For the Lord our God the Almighty reigns" (Rev. 19:6). In between these visions of the beginning and end of history, the Bible proclaims the mighty deeds of God. The psalmist sings praises to God the Creator and Redeemer: "Great is our Lord, and abundant in power" (Ps. 147:5).

But what is this power that the Bible ascribes to God? Can we express it in a single sentence? Or does the Bible speak in many ways and in many voices about the power of God? Do these many voices sometimes stand in tension with one another and even at times seem to contradict one another? The answer is yes, the Bible contains a chorus of voices rather than one solitary voice. Israel's faith in God developed over many centuries, and as a result there are many strands in the Old Testament tradition. We are thus presented not with a single image of God and God's power but with a rich diversity of images. Often the diversity contributes to a fuller understanding of the power of God. Sometimes the diverse voices seem to clash with one another and are not easily brought into harmony.

Israel shared many beliefs about God with its neighbors of the ancient Near East. Like them, Israel could associate God's power with the phenomena of storm, lightning, and thunder. Like them, Israel could speak of God's power in the awesome vitality of nature and in the fertility of plants, animals, and human beings. Israel, too, could praise the power of the warrior God and declare God's superiority in battle.

But we would not yet grasp what is distinctive in Israel's faith in God by focusing on these aspects of the Old Testament tradition. What stand out in its witness to the reality and power of God are the following elements.

1. The power of God is sung and celebrated by Israel first and foremost in the story of *God's surprising liberation of a poor and oppressed people.* The core confession of the Old Testament—"The LORD brought us out of Egypt with a mighty hand" (Deut. 26:5–9)—narrates the exodus of the people of Israel from bondage in Egypt by the power of God. God is the exodus God. The power of God sets free those in bondage. We cannot overstate the revolutionary character of this experience and this description of God's power. In this event, the power of God is distinguished from oppressive, authoritarian power. If God is the exodus God, the power of God is manifested in bringing new freedom and new life to a world of bondage. This stunning redefinition of divine power appears not in the form of a philosophical discourse but in the form of historical narrative. "I am the LORD your God, who brought you out of the land of Egypt, out of the house of slavery" (Exod. 20:2). God's power is liberating power. It is known decisively in an event that issues in religious, political, social, and economic liberation.

2. While the depiction of God as exodus-liberating God is of great importance, it does not stand alone in the Old Testament. It is deepened and enriched by other dimensions of God's activity. The God who liberates an oppressed people also establishes a covenant with them. God promises to be faithful to them and in turn calls the people to faithfulness. "I will take you as my people, and I will be your God" (Exod. 6:7; Jer. 30:22). Through Moses, God gives his law to the people of Israel to order their life and to establish justice and peace in their everyday relationships. Thus according to the biblical witness, the power of God is not only liberating; it also *demands justice and creates order.* It is both a power that grants freedom to those in bondage and a power that calls for justice on the earth. This two-sidedness of God's power—the gift of freedom and the call to justice that accompanies this gift—is an unmistakable feature of the Old Testament witness. The liberty that God wills for all creatures is not anarchic or self-centered. It is made concrete in the practice of justice and regard for the welfare of others, especially the poor and the weak.

The Old Testament does not present the history of the people of Israel after the exodus as trouble free. Wandering in the desert, the people yearn to return to the bondage they knew in Egypt, where at least they had bread to eat. There are other times when the people find the commandments of God too hard to follow. They go their own way, fall into idolatry, and ignore the call for justice.

That God's power is a justice-demanding and order-creating power is central to the message of the great prophets of Israel. "[Israel] judged the cause of the poor and needy; then it was well. Is not this to know me? says the LORD" (Jer. 22:16). "He has told you, O mortal, what is good; and what does the LORD require of you but to do justice, and to love kindness, and to walk humbly with your God?" (Mic. 6:8). The prophets never tire of warning that the liberating power of God is abused and corrupted if it is not seen as the foundation of justice in human life. To know the exodus God—the God who sets prisoners free—is to do justice.

Rooted in the events of exodus and Sinai, the faith of Israel expands to include affirmation of God's sovereignty over all nations and over the whole creation. Just as Israel owes its existence to the Lord who created a people out of a group of "nobodies" enslaved by a world empire, so all peoples and all creation have come into being by the sheer grace of their creator. God's grace and call to justice extend through Israel to all the nations of the earth. The book of Jonah teaches that God wants not only Israel but all nations to repent and experience new life. Thus, far from being a provincial deity, the redeemer of Israel is the Lord of all nations and the creator of heaven and earth (Gen. 1:1ff.). God is "God of gods" and "Lord of lords" (Ps. 136:2–3). God's liberating and justice-making power encompasses the whole world.

3. If God's liberating power includes the call to justice, it is also *merciful power*. The hallmark of the God of the Old Testament, and especially of the prophets, is not sheer almightiness but mercy and steadfast love (*hesed*). The steadfast love of God is a prominent theme of the prophets and the psalmist (Pss. 23:6; 100:5). Although still popular in some quarters, it is a complete distortion to contrast the God of the Old Testament, as a God of raw and unforgiving power, with the God of the New Testament, as a God of tender love and infinite mercy. According to the Old Testament, God's power is inseparably bound up with his steadfast love for his people. The God of Israel is especially concerned with the plight of people who are poor, weak, and easily abused—widows, orphans, strangers in the land. Just as God heard the cries of Israel in bondage in Egypt, so God continues

to hear the cries of the poor and the oppressed. God has compassion on these helpless people and warns of judgment if justice is not done on their behalf.

God's steadfast love reaches out to people in their sin, in their forgetfulness of the freedom bestowed on them, and in their violation of the justice demanded of them. Unlike other gods, the God of Israel shows power in the form of mercy and forgiveness. "Who is a God like you, pardoning iniquity and passing over the transgression of the remnant of your possession? He does not retain his anger forever, because he delights in showing clemency" (Mic. 7:18). God's compassion is like that of a mother for her beloved children (Isa. 66:12ff.). The refusal of God to give up on his beloved people and to endure and forgive their disobedience brings grief and suffering to God.[5] The theme of the faithful and long-suffering parental love of God is beautifully expressed by the prophet Hosea:

> When Israel was a child, I loved him,
>     and out of Egypt I called my son.
> The more I called them,
>     the more they went from me;
> they kept sacrificing to the Baals,
>     and offering incense to idols.
> Yet it was I who taught Ephraim to walk,
>     I took them up in my arms;
>     but they did not know that I healed them.
> I led them with cords of human kindness,
>     with bands of love.
> I was to them like those
>     who lift infants to their cheeks.
>     I bent down to them and fed them. . . .
>
> How can I give you up, Ephraim?
>     How can I hand you over, O Israel?
> How can I make you like Admah?
>     How can I treat you like Zeboiim?
> My heart recoils within me,
>     my compassion grows warm and tender.
> I will not execute my fierce anger;
>     I will not again destroy Ephraim;

for I am God and no mortal,
  the Holy One in your midst,
  and I will not come in wrath.
                          (Hos. 11:1–4, 8–9)

4. The Old Testament witness to the exodus God, who calls for justice and exercises steadfast love, shatters all ideas of God as author and administrator of oppressive rule. Or does it? Are there not "texts of violence" in the Old Testament witness?[6] What about those who are killed or displaced in the event of the exodus and in the invasion and conquest of the land promised by God to the people of Israel? What about God's call to slay the enemies of Israel, even to destroy them to the last man, woman, child, and beast (1 Sam. 15:3)? What about the prayer of the psalmist that the little children of his enemies may be dashed against the rocks (Ps. 137:9)? Are these stories and pictures of a liberating, justice-making, compassionate God?

This is a very difficult topic and one that disturbs all thoughtful readers and hearers of the Bible. I can say only a few things here, and these all too briefly. First, we should not pretend that these deeply troubling texts of the Bible do not exist. We should not evade them or try to smooth them over by giving them "spiritual" interpretations. In earlier centuries, a text like Psalm 137:9 was explained by saying that when the psalmist prays that the heads of the children of the enemies of Israel be crushed on the rocks, this is a mystical reference to our sinful thoughts that must be nipped in the bud. Most readers of the Bible today would no longer find this a convincing response to the problem posed by such texts.

Second, we have a responsibility to understand these difficult biblical passages, like all biblical texts, in their historical contexts. In what circumstances were these texts composed and what did they intend to say to their original readers or hearers? Is the anguished cry for justice also to be heard in these texts?

Third, we should recognize that simply because certain events are reported in the Bible does not mean we are required to endorse them uncritically. In his anger and grief over the savage treatment of the children of his own people, the psalmist has given in to the desire for revenge and retaliation. It is not said, however, that God approves of this attitude, and it is not presented as an ethical norm to guide our lives.

Fourth, it would be self-deception to consider ourselves beyond the attitudes and practices described in these texts and to conclude that we do not need to be addressed by them and can simply excise them from the Bible. What do these texts have to say to us? They confront us with the depth of human violence and brutality that we modern readers cannot claim to be free of. If what the psalmist wished for the children of his enemies was indeed horrible, "was it any more horrible than the practices of modern warfare, of throwing napalm on the naked bodies of little children in Vietnam, of saturation bombing . . . , of chemical warfare . . . , of the creation of hell on earth for the children of Hiroshima?"[7] Or was it more horrible, we might add, than the killing of children by suicide bombers, or as the "collateral damage" of antiterrorist wars in Afghanistan and Iraq?

Finally, and most importantly, we have to remember that we are addressed by God through the Bible as a whole and not piecemeal through isolated texts. If there are texts of violence in the Bible, there are also texts that speak against the way of violence and even look forward to a time when violence will be removed from God's creation. The issue is not one of New Testament versus Old Testament. In the Old Testament as well as the New, there are passages that call for love of enemies, of feeding them if they are hungry and giving them water to drink if they are thirsty (Prov. 25:21; Rom. 12:20), rather than living by the law of retaliation. There are also many Old Testament texts that tell of God's promise of a world where violence is absent. "They will not hurt or destroy on all my holy mountain; for the earth will be full of the knowledge of the LORD as the waters cover the sea" (Isa. 11:9).[8]

5. In addition to the justice and compassion of God that are associated with God's liberating power, the *promise of God* is also part of the Old Testament witness to the identity and power of God. The life-giving power of God is experienced both as a reality and as a promise. Liberation has come, and yet it needs to come again and in still greater depth and scope. Justice is sometimes experienced, but more often injustice, exploitation, and cruelty reign. The compassion of God is now and then an experienced reality, but all too often there is also the

terrible experience of the absence and silence of God. Peace sometimes prevails but violence more often rules the day. The Old Testament knows joy but also lamentation and affliction. Israel thus yearns for the full realization of God's justice, peace, and freedom in all the earth. This yearning is unforgettably expressed in the book of Job, in the cries of the psalmists, and in the visions and prayers of the prophets. "Surely his salvation is at hand. . . . Steadfast love and faithfulness will meet; righteousness and peace will kiss each other" (Ps. 85:9–10). "They shall beat their swords into plowshares . . . ; nation shall not lift up sword against nation, neither shall they learn war any more" (Isa. 2:4). "I am about to create new heavens and a new earth; the former things shall not be remembered or come to mind" (Isa. 65:17). The Old Testament proclaims the exodus God, and it looks forward with burning anticipation to a new and greater exodus from bondage and to a world where the justice and peace (*shalom*) of God prevail everywhere.

### The Power of the Crucified and Risen Christ

Just as there are many voices in the Old Testament that speak of the power of God, there are also many voices in the New Testament that proclaim "the power of God for salvation" (Rom. 1:16) in the person and work of Jesus Christ. In addition to the four Gospels, each with its particular emphases, the New Testament also contains a number of apostolic letters written to different congregations and speaking to particular issues. Yet amid this diversity, there are common elements in the New Testament witness to Jesus as the definitive revelation and personal embodiment of the reconciling power of God.

The God of the Old Testament and the God of the New Testament are one and the same God. Jesus does not proclaim a new God but the very same God who liberated Israel from bondage, gave the law to Moses, and spoke through the prophets. The God and Father of Jesus Christ is none other than the God praised by Israel. As with the Old Testament, we can identify several distinctive elements of the New Testament witness to the purpose and power of God.

1. Jesus announces *the inbreaking of the reign of God.* He declares that the rule of the holy God of Israel is on the threshold. The God

who rules justly and graciously over the whole creation, sending rain on the just and the unjust (Matt. 5:45), feeding the birds of the air, and adorning the lilies of the field (Matt. 6:26ff.), is acting to make all things right. With urgency Jesus summons his hearers to respond to the boundless goodness, mercy, and forgiveness of God by repenting, giving thanks to God, loving God with all their heart, soul, mind, and strength, and loving their neighbors as themselves (Mark 12:28–31).

Who God is and what the lordly rule of God is like are made known by Jesus not only in his teachings but also in his actions. He teaches with astonishing authority (Mark 1:22), but he does more. In the power of the Spirit, he also casts out demons (v. 27), heals the sick (vv. 30–31), and raises the dead (John 11:38–44). He proclaims good news to the poor (Luke 6:20), announces the long-awaited day of liberation to those in bondage (Luke 4:18–19), and dares to forgive sins on God's behalf (Mark 2:1–12). He befriends women and has table fellowship with sinners, tax collectors, and other despised people. The reign of God—the renewing, transforming power of God—is breaking into every corner of human life in Jesus' mighty deeds and in his ministry of forgiveness of sins.

2. The liberating words and actions of Jesus bring him into *collision with the religious and political leaders of the day.* The disturbance caused by Jesus' ministry is evident in many episodes in the Gospels. In the stories of conflicts about Sabbath observance, the opponents of Jesus insist that the Sabbath is the day reserved strictly for the honor of God. Even deeds of helping the needy are declared by some to be forbidden on the Sabbath. Jesus contends, on the contrary, that God is honored where humanity is set free. It is proper to do good on the Sabbath because "the sabbath was made for humankind, and not humankind for the sabbath" (Mark 2:27). In this Sabbath debate as well as in the other conflicts of Jesus with his opponents, the central controversy comes to light—whether God is a power of repression and fear or a liberating force in the midst of life. The God whose coming kingdom Jesus proclaims wants people to be free. Jesus empowers the powerless by extending to them God's forgiveness and acceptance. He tells the "nobodies" of his time that they are "somebodies" in God's eyes. God's gift of dignity-granting forgiveness flows freely from Jesus' proclamation and ministry.

Jesus does not proclaim and serve a God of the social and religious status quo. His message and ministry run counter to those who have turned God into an instrument of self-righteous exclusion and used God's law as a legalistic weapon of oppression. He boldly calls God "Abba" ("dear father") (Mark 14:36) and teaches his disciples to address God as "Our Father in heaven" (Matt. 6:9). As noted previously, this way of addressing God is an expression of Jesus' own intimate relationship with God and a sign of a different understanding of divine power embodied in his life and ministry. The God Jesus calls "Father" is not a God who oppresses but a God who calls for justice and freely offers mercy and forgiveness.

The proclamation of the extravagant love and costly forgiveness of God that sets people free is beautifully portrayed in the parable of the Prodigal Son (Luke 15:11–32). In this parable a father allows his son to go off on his own. Having squandered the family inheritance in loose living and now finding himself in abject poverty, the son has a change of heart and returns home in shame. Even before he is asked, the awaiting father is eager to forgive his son. He runs out to meet him and lavishes gifts on him. God's power, the parable teaches, is not like that of a vindictive despot but like that of a caring parent. Redefining the power of God in this way creates anger and resentment among those who hear the parable. They react like the elder brother of the parable who bitterly resents the forgiveness and joy with which the younger brother is welcomed home.

What Jesus teaches in this parable of the surprising and abundant grace of God, he enacts in his ministry to the poor, the unwanted, and the castoffs of this world. They are welcomed into God's kingdom. Jesus infuriates his opponents with his ministry of God's generosity because it challenges their lifeworld. Their own exercise of power is questioned by his message and ministry of forgiveness. Their understanding of God and God's power that supports their personal and corporate practices is shaken to the foundations.

Jesus' teaching and ministry deeply disturb both those in positions of power and their adversaries. The Jewish and Roman leaders are threatened in different ways by his message of a new kingdom of justice and freedom. "He has blasphemed!" the high priest charges (Matt. 26:65). "Are you the King of the Jews?" Pilate asks anxiously.

But Jesus is also disturbing to the Zealots, who advocate violence to achieve independence from Rome. He refuses to take up the sword in armed revolt against the Roman occupation forces. He is not a political revolutionary, nor does he form a political party to achieve social and political change. When Jesus is asked whether taxes should be paid to Caesar, he replies, "Give . . . to the emperor the things that are the emperor's, and to God the things that are God's" (Matt. 22:21). In his answer, Jesus recognizes a relative and limited authority of the rulers of this world. At the same time, he clearly differentiates between the allegiance that is owed earthly rulers and the greater allegiance that is owed God. Talk of an inbreaking reign of God marked by forgiveness and love of enemy discredits both the Roman reliance on brute force and the hatred of the Jewish nationalists for their Roman oppressors.

In his message and ministry, and in the opposition that it arouses, it is clear that Jesus embodies a revolutionary change in the meaning and exercise of power. He tells his disciples: "Rulers [of the Gentiles] lord it over them. . . . But whoever wishes to become great among you must be your servant" (Mark 10:42–45). He reminds them, "I am among you as one who serves" (Luke 22:27). True power is not in domination but in service of others. The ultimate power is not the power of the master over the slave but the power of justice, forgiveness, and self-giving love.

3. Jesus' message of God's grace and forgiveness is at the same time a *message of divine judgment*. The grace of God is not to be trivialized or taken as a matter of course. Human beings are faced with the loss of God's intended goal for them and the entire creation when they persist in resistance to the coming of God's reign of justice and mercy. Yet if the grace of God is not to be separated from his judgment, neither is God's judgment to be separated from his grace. As in the Old Testament, so in the proclamation and ministry of Jesus, the judgment of God is never torn apart from the gracious purposes of God and made an independent theme in its own right.

Equally important, Jesus forbids his disciples to take the judgment of God into their own hands. They are warned against assigning to themselves the authority to render final judgment on others, let alone attempting to carry out that judgment. The holy and gracious God alone is judge. Jesus calls his disciples to relinquish all self-righteousness and every spirit of vindictiveness. Hatred of enemy is to be replaced by love. The apostle Paul teaches the same: "Beloved, never avenge yourselves, but leave room for the wrath of God; for it is written, 'Vengeance is mine, I will repay, says the Lord.' No, 'if your enemies are hungry, feed them; if they are thirsty, give them something to drink; for by doing this you will heap burning coals on their heads.' Do not be overcome by evil, but overcome evil with good" (Rom. 12:19–21).

4. The opposition that Jesus' message and ministry create eventually conspires to bring about his *crucifixion*. The question of true power is clearly at issue at several points in the passion narrative. At his arrest, Jesus refuses to allow his disciples to defend him with the sword (Matt. 26:52). God's saving purposes are not accomplished by the power of the sword. At his trial, Pilate asks whether Jesus knows he has power to crucify him. Jesus responds that whatever power Pilate has comes from God and is limited. Implied in this response is that rulers of this world can abuse the power they have been given by God, but God's own power is greater still. The power of God's reign that Jesus proclaims and embodies is different from and greater than the finite powers of this world that are frequently abused (John 18:33ff.; 19:8ff.).

Crucified between two political prisoners, Jesus dies as he lived— in utmost solidarity with the lost and despised of this world. What Jesus' death means cannot be rightly grasped apart from his life and ministry. Jesus, the Son of God, dies on a cross in faithfulness to his divinely given mission of conquering the sinful powers of this world with the different power of God's forgiving love. Like nothing else, the event of the cross forever shatters the equation of divine power with oppressive rule and self-aggrandizing mastery over others. This is vividly expressed in one of the scenes under the cross. Those surrounding the dying Jesus mock him with the words: "He saved others; let him save himself" (Luke 23:35–37, 39). We might paraphrase these words as follows: "Show us that you have the power to save yourself, to survive, to look out for number one, and then we will believe that you can also help us. For we want to survive above all else, and we acknowledge power that is useful to that end." The conception of power held by those who mock Jesus is exactly the bondage from which he wants to set them free. Their conception of power is totally centered on themselves. In his suffering and death as in his ministry, Jesus refuses to invoke the power of God in a way that would merely support the dominant and dehumanizing ideas of divine and human power. He refuses to play the power games of this world. He turns away from the never-ending cycle of violence against violence. He does not respond to injury with a vow of vengeance. From the cross he prays, "Father, forgive them; for they do not know what they are doing" (Luke 23:34).

The New Testament witnesses are painfully honest in describing how little of this the disciples understood until after Jesus was raised from the dead. When Jesus explains that he will have to suffer and die, Peter did not want to hear anything like this and had to be rebuked by Jesus (Mark 8:31–33). On the way to Jerusalem and the final days of Jesus' life, some of his disciples approach him with the request that they be given special places of honor in his coming kingdom. The disciples are obviously still thinking of the power of God as imperial rule, in which they are eager to share.

5. For the New Testament witnesses, what is astonishingly new in all that Jesus says and does is that he is God's own "Son," God with us, the eternal Word of God made human (John 1:14), "the image of the invisible God" (Col. 1:15), the power and wisdom of God (1 Cor. 1:24). If the key image of God in the Old Testament is the event of the exodus, the key image of God and God's power in the New Testament is a person, Jesus of Nazareth—what he does, what he suffers, what comes of his life.

Among the New Testament writers, it is Paul who ponders most deeply the way in which *Jesus' suffering, death, and resurrection redefine the power of God*. Paul knows well and takes with utmost seriousness the violent powers of this world—the coercive "power of sin" (Rom. 3:9) and the oppressive reign of death (Rom. 5:14). In the light of the cross of Christ, however, Paul declares an even greater power. God has shown his power in a completely unexpected form. This man Jesus, crucified in weakness, is the Lord. What to human eyes is shameful, weak, and ineffective is God's own glory and strength. In a startling phrase, Paul proclaims "God's weakness" (1 Cor. 1:25). This is an unprecedented way of speaking of the power of God, and it yields a highly paradoxical account of true power. The power of God made known in the cross of Christ is stronger than all human might.

According to Paul, the weakness of God that is stronger than human strength is the power of atonement, forgiveness, and reconciliation: "In Christ God was reconciling the world to himself" (2 Cor. 5:19). What does reconciliation mean? It means at-one-ment between God and humanity. It means that God's astonishing act of forgiveness in Jesus Christ has created the basis of a new relationship between God and humanity. It means that in Jesus Christ God has done all that is needed to restore a right relationship between God and humanity and among human beings. The reconciliation of God and humanity does not come cheap. Reconciliation means that in Christ God has taken to himself all the consequences of our sinful, violent ways and all the judgment that we should have borne. Without the gift of God's forgiving love—the "weak" power of God—humanity would be lost in its slavery to sin and death, lost in its enslavement to ways of injustice and violence.

Note well: Jesus and his cross are not for Paul, or for any other New Testament witness, the way by which an angry God is pacified. How could that possibly manifest the power of God as altogether different from the power of control and domination? While all that Jesus does and suffers is part of God's purpose of redemption (Eph. 1:3–10), God does not demand the death of Jesus as a condition of forgiveness. The demand for Jesus' crucifixion comes from the Roman authorities, the religious leaders, and the crowds. The Son of God wills to give life in abundance (John 10:10), even to the point of freely giving his life for us on the cross.

Critics of the gospel say that to speak of God's power as decisively revealed in the life and death of Jesus, in his act of self-giving, in his gift of forgiveness, is to limit and "soften" God's power, to cheapen and sentimentalize God's grace. Paul is well aware of these objections, but for him what God has accomplished for us in Christ is majestic and costly, not small and cheap.

For Paul, the good news is that in Jesus Christ God freely and graciously entered into the depths of our human condition, with all its sin, violence, and suffering. In his incarnation, death, and resurrection, God took on himself the divine judgment on the power of sin that invariably violates God, our neighbors, and ourselves. Jesus Christ is not the victim of an angry God; he is God with us as one of us, graciously taking the fury of our sin and violent ways on himself. We only come to a full realization of the seriousness of sin and the violence that accompanies it when we are confronted by the suffering that it costs God to remove.

From New Testament times to the present, the scandalous story of the crucified God has shaken to the foundations all preconceptions of divine power. The shock produced by the picture of a crucified Lord is movingly portrayed by the Swedish writer Pär Lagerkvist in his novel *Barabbas*. At one point in the story, an overseer questions a Christian slave named Sahak about his faith.

> "—The only God! And crucified like a slave! What presumption! Do you mean that there is supposed to be only one God, and that people crucified him!"
>
> —"Yes," Sahak said. "That is how it is."
>
> The man gazed at him dumbfounded.[9]

6. If we take the drama of the gospel to heart, our understanding of God and the nature of true power must change. We know that it radically changed the life of Paul. It transformed him from a persecutor of the church into its most energetic missionary. In his own experience he learned that the power of God is "made perfect in weakness" (2 Cor. 12:9). In his ministry he discovered the power of the gospel to break down the barriers between humanity and God, between Jews and Gentiles, men and women, slaves and masters (Gal. 3:28). For Paul the "weakness of God" manifest on the cross is nothing less than "the power of God for salvation" (Rom. 1:16) and is stronger than death itself. As he writes in his letter to the church at Rome (at that time, the power center of the world), nothing in all creation, "neither death, nor life, nor angels, nor rulers, nor things present, nor things to come, nor powers, nor height, nor depth . . . will be able to separate us from the love of God in Christ Jesus our Lord" (Rom. 8:38–39).

As these affirmations of Paul show, he knows well that the "weakness of God" manifest so shockingly on the cross is far from powerless. At the heart of Paul's gospel is the affirmation that God raised the crucified Jesus from the dead (1 Cor. 15:3–4). Jesus is not dead but alive by the power of God (Eph. 1:20). The Spirit sent from God by the risen Lord is in the world today continuing the work that Jesus inaugurated. God's Spirit is the *dynamis,* the power or energy of new beginnings in human life. As the power of God at work among us, the Holy Spirit bears witness to all that Jesus has said and done, unites us to him, breaks our bondage to self-centeredness and exploitation of others, and frees us for a new life of inclusive friendship and community with God and our fellow human beings. Where the Spirit of the Lord is, there is liberty (2 Cor. 3:17). Where the Spirit is at work, there is the beginning of a new community in which each member is gifted and valued. Of course, this power of the Spirit of God at work in us is not our possession, not ours to boast about or to use as we please. It comes from and belongs to God and is to serve God's purposes (2 Cor. 4:7).

To be moved by the Spirit of resurrection and new life is to undergo a *metanoia*, a conversion, a complete turnaround in one's understanding of power and in one's exercise of power. Nothing in one's daily life and practice is left undisturbed. The power of God present in Jesus and still at work by his Spirit is the power of forgiveness of sins, of love of the enemy, of solidarity with the oppressed, of the passion for justice and reconciliation. God's power is truly different. Neither brute force nor subtle coercion has anything to do with the power of God. The power of God's Spirit brings a beginning, a "first fruits," here and now of a new freedom, a new life rooted in forgiveness, a new community of people once estranged from God and divided from one another. It is no more than a beginning, but it is a beginning that gives birth to hope. It awakens hope for the completion of God's purposes for the entire creation. Jesus is risen and will return in glory. Just as the Old Testament eagerly awaits a new and fuller deliverance by the exodus God, so the New Testament looks forward eagerly to the consummation in all creation of the new life in freedom, justice, and friendship centered in the crucified and risen Lord.

7. If we are attentive to the New Testament witness, we will discern a *threefold pattern* in the way it speaks of the power of God. This threefold pattern has a narrative form, and it is the biblical root of the later Christian doctrine of the Trinity. The central figure of the narrative is the person of Jesus—his ministry, cross, and resurrection. But the Jesus of the gospel narrative is not an isolated figure. He is always

related to the one who sent him, the one he calls Father. He is also always related to the life-giving Spirit who is at work in his ministry and who, after the crucifixion and resurrection, is sent to bear witness to Jesus. We can summarize the New Testament witness in the following way: the Son of God sent by the Father is present in human form in the person of Jesus and continues to work through his liberating, life-transforming Spirit. According to the New Testament, the activity of Father, Son, and Holy Spirit defines who God is and the nature of the power God exercises.

God is the transcendent Lord who at great cost sends Jesus on his mission of salvation. God is the humble servant who faithfully does the will of the Father and gives himself even unto death so that all of God's creatures might be free from every bondage. God is the life-renewing and life-transforming Spirit who bears witness to the self-giving love of the Father and the Son and who, as the "pledge" (2 Cor. 1:22) and "first fruits" (Rom. 8:23) of God's coming kingdom, is the power to complete all the purposes of God. Thus the power of God—the power of creative, suffering, transforming love—has a Trinitarian shape according to the New Testament witness. The doctrine of the Trinity expresses a radically new understanding of the majestic power of God. It is the omnipotence of God's free grace made known in the crucified and risen Jesus and in the activity of his life-transforming Spirit.

Later I will say more about the doctrine of the Trinity as the distinctively Christian understanding of God. But before doing that, we need to examine an influential strand of traditional Christian theology in which a radical rethinking of the power of God in the light of the biblical witness is missing. We also need to ask to what extent the church's exercise of power in its own life has obscured the gospel proclamation of the difference between God's power, decisively revealed in the weakness and foolishness of the cross, and the understanding and use of power that marks our world.

## Questions for Discussion

1. Why do you agree or disagree with the claim that Jesus Christ is the key to a proper reading of the Bible?

2. Explain why it is a mistake to say the Old Testament views God as a God of wrath while the New Testament views God as a God of love.
3. In what way does the crucifixion of Jesus Christ, the Son of God, call for a rethinking of the meaning of the omnipotence of God?
4. How do you understand the "weakness of God"?

# 4

# The Power of God in the Theology and Life of the Church

*The kings of the Gentiles lord it over them . . . but not so with you*
(Luke 22:25–26)

## The Attributes of God in Christian Theology

In the previous chapter we surveyed the biblical witness to the power of God. Divine power is described there in a way that shatters many of our assumptions. It is not the power of totalitarian rule but the power of the exodus God who acts to liberate a people in bondage. It is not the power of sheer almightiness but the healing and reconciling power at work in the ministry, death, and resurrection of Jesus Christ. Jesus forgives sinners, heals the sick, preaches good news to the poor, and finally suffers and dies to reconcile the world with God. Paul can talk of this power of God in the crucified Jesus as "weak," yet paradoxically stronger than all human power.

God's different power at work in Jesus' ministry, death, and resurrection did not cease after his return to his Father. The risen and living Christ continues to work by his Spirit, who bears witness to what Christ has accomplished, brings new life and freedom, and builds new community. While the power of God as creator and sustainer of the world is not limited to the events attested by the scriptural witness, it is here, especially in the gospel narrative, that Christian faith finds most transparent the true nature and purpose of God's power. The power of God is different.

According to some theologians, the history of the church can be understood as the history of the church's interpretation of Scripture. We might modify this idea a bit by saying that the history of the church can be understood as a history in which the message of Scripture has been both understood and misunderstood. This becomes clear when we trace the modifications of the biblical witness to the power of God in the history of Christian theology and in the life of the church.

In a note discovered after his death, Blaise Pascal, the great seventeenth-century scientist and philosopher, recorded an intense religious experience that changed his life. He provided few details of what happened other than to say it was like "fire." In this experience Pascal became completely certain of the reality of God. While Pascal was far from being a despiser of reason and philosophy, the God whom he knew with certainty in his fiery experience was "God of Abraham, God of Isaac, God of Jacob, not of the philosophers and scholars." For Pascal the living God is the God of the biblical witness: "God of Jesus Christ. . . . He is to be found only by the ways taught in the Gospel. . . . We keep hold of him only by the ways taught in the Gospel."[1]

Pascal's sharp contrast between the God of the biblical witness and the God of philosophical reason touches an exposed nerve in the history of the Christian understanding of God. Through the centuries many Christians have felt the same tension experienced so acutely by Pascal. In its theology and in its life the church has wavered back and forth between an understanding of God heavily indebted to the classical philosophical conceptions of Absolute Being and an understanding of God derived from the story of Jesus.

After the crucifixion, the disciples of Jesus experienced utter defeat and "total powerlessness."[2] However, with the resurrection of Jesus and the outpouring of his Spirit, the disciples proclaimed the message of the crucified and risen Lord with zest and joy. Their previous understandings of the power of God had been radically changed by Jesus' death and resurrection. The mission of the early church depended solely on the power of the Word and Spirit of God (1 Cor. 2:4).

In the *Letter to Diognetus* written in the early part of the third century, the author shows that he has a firm hold on the significance of the cross for our understanding of the power of God. Responding to the question of why God sent his Son to the world, the author replies:

"to rule by tyranny, fear, and terror? Far from it! He sent him out of kindness and gentleness, like a king sending his son who is himself a king. He sent him as God; he sent him as man to men. He willed to save man by persuasion, not by compulsion, for compulsion is not God's way of working."[3]

As the church continued to expand from its Palestinian beginnings into the Hellenistic world, the biblical message had to be expressed in new terms. To better articulate and defend the faith in its new context the church made use of the categories of ancient Greek metaphysics. The biblical story of God's creative and redemptive activity was recast in the metaphysical conceptuality that was then current. In this process the church both gained and lost. The gain was twofold. First, the philo-sophical categories were familiar to the intelligentsia of that time. This made it easier for the church to communicate its teaching in an under-standable form. Second, classical philosophy enabled the church to express the universality of God's lordship. By speaking of the God of the biblical witness with such terms as *Pantocrator*—the power that controls all things—the church prevented its witness from becoming the story of a local or provincial deity. It would thus be unfair to fault the early church for making use of the philosophical categories at its disposal in order to communicate its message as effectively as possi ble. The proclamation of the Christian gospel in different times and cultures has always necessarily involved a translation process.

Nevertheless, there was loss as well as gain in this process. We have to ask whether the church's appropriation of the metaphysical categories of its time was sufficiently self-critical. Did the conceptu-ality that was adopted to help in the understanding and communicat-ing of the biblical witness subtly alter its message? Put starkly, did the biblical message absorb and transform the metaphysics, or did the metaphysics absorb and domesticate the biblical message?

This question continues to be debated among theologians. Some say the church's message was "hellenized" with serious consequences. Others say the notion of the "hellenization" of the gospel is a mis-reading of what happened. They claim that far from abandoning its message to Hellenistic culture, the church Christianized the culture. Both of these positions contain a grain of truth. What we can say with certainty is that the recasting of the biblical witness in metaphysical categories gave rise to new questions about the church's language of the power of God. The tension between diverging views of power within the Christian tradition is perhaps best seen in the doctrine of God as presented in scholastic forms of Christian theology.

By "scholastic theology" I mean those schools of Christian theology, prominent in the later Middle Ages and in the post-Reformation period, in which a metaphysical approach to the understanding of God gained a relative independence from the biblical witness.[4] This led to ways of thinking and speaking of God that, measured by the biblical witness, were at best one-sided.

How did scholastic theology describe the God of the Bible? What attributes of God were given the greatest attention? What methods were employed in speaking of God?

One way of speaking of God prominent in scholastic theology is *negation*. We speak of God properly when we say that God is *not* something in this world. God is not a creature. God is not finite (God is in-finite), not mortal (God is im-mortal), not changeable (God is im-mutable). Another way of speaking of God in scholastic theology is the way of *eminence*. We can speak responsibly of God by beginning with what is good and laudable in creatures and then ascribing the highest degree of these virtues to God. Thus God is not only wise but maximally wise, all-knowing (omniscient), not only present here or there but present everywhere (omnipresent), not only powerful but all-powerful (omnipotent). Still another way of speaking of God in scholastic theology is the way of *analogy*. Analogy combines similarity and difference. There is both likeness and unlikeness between the attributes of creatures and the attributes of God. To speak of God as father or mother, for example, is to speak analogically. God is like a human parent, but also very different from our experience of our own parents or our own ways of being parents.

These ways of speaking of God—negative, positive, and analogical—are in some form or other employed in all Christian theology. They are helpful and even unavoidable. At best, they are efforts to protect the otherness of God, to guard against the domestication of God, to acknowledge the incomprehensibility of God. However, the more these ways of speaking of God become independent of the biblical story, the more they fall short of a distinctively Christian understanding of God.

We find the influence of scholastic descriptions of God in a familiar hymn like "Immortal, Invisible, God Only Wise":

> Immortal, invisible, God only wise,
>   In light inaccessible hid from our eyes,
> Most blessed, most glorious, the Ancient of Days,
>   Almighty, victorious, Thy great name we praise.

The following stanzas of this hymn speak of God as beyond every want and as immune to all change. While not simply false, the affirmations of this hymn leave an overall impression of the greatness of God that is one-sided. Left unqualified, the divine attributes that are stressed tend to obscure what is distinctive of the God of the biblical witness. By themselves, they seem unable adequately to describe God as revealed in Jesus. God is indeed "immortal," but in Jesus Christ the Son of God has suffered and died for us. God is indeed light "inaccessible," but in Jesus Christ the light of God has shone in our darkness.

Consider more closely some of the attributes of God as defined by scholastic theology. Most important is *omnipotence*. How is this term to be understood when it is used of God? For scholastic theology omnipotence means all-powerfulness. God is able to do anything, except of course what is self-contradictory. God cannot create a round square or make two plus two equal five (these are simply nonsense). Beyond this, however, all conceivable power belongs to God. While a theology faithful to the Bible must say this, it must say far more, or say it differently. The problem is that if omnipotence is abstracted from the gospel story, it comes to mean simply God-almightiness. The power of God is then the greatest power imaginable. What can possibly be wrong in ascribing the greatest power to God? To this we must reply that we have not yet been told what true power is. Thinking of the greatest power as simply the magnification of power as understood and practiced by finite, sinful creatures encourages a quantitative way of thinking and speaking of God. A child has a little power; an adult has more power; a king has a huge amount of power; God has the most power of all.

The biblical witness does not speak of God's power in this way. It describes the power of God the creator who gives and preserves the life of creatures. It describes the power of God the redeemer who judges and saves his people. But this power of God is altogether different from mere almightiness. According to the prophet Zechariah, God says, "Not by might, nor by power, but by my spirit" (Zech. 4:6). As we have seen, the decisive depiction of the power of God in the New Testament is the story of the passion and resurrection of Christ. The approach of scholastic theology tends to lose this narrative approach of the Bible and instead speaks of God's powerfulness in abstract speculation about all the things God can or cannot do. Let me be clear: the intention of scholastic theology is laudable. It wants to give God all the glory. But the crucified Jesus Christ, who is God with us, does not fit into a speculative framework. This story demands a complete overhaul of our thinking about power. God is certainly the supreme power. But this does not mean that we have said what is most important when we declare that God is "all the power there is," or that "God can do anything."

It is no accident that in the Apostles' Creed the church confesses its faith not in divine almightiness in general but in God the *Father* "almighty." This refers us at once to the gospel story. It is God the Father of our Lord Jesus Christ who establishes the true meaning of "almighty" or "omnipotent." Karl Barth reminds us that Adolf Hitler was fond of speaking of God as "the Almighty."[5] Power in itself, mere almightiness, might better describe the power of the demonic rather than the power of God. Scholastic theology defines God's omnipotence in a one-sided manner that easily leads to distortion. According to the Bible, God is omnipotent in the sense that God has all the power needed to create, redeem, and complete the world in a personal and noncoercive way. The power of God made known in Jesus Christ is not sheer omnipotence but omnipotent love that judges and redeems.

Another important attribute of God in scholastic theology is *immutability*. The literal meaning of immutability is changelessness. God does not move, or undergo change, or have a history. God is not in process of becoming more fully God. God is perfect, and what is perfect never changes or becomes something other than it was before. If what is perfect changed, it could only change for the better (in which case it was not perfect before) or for the worse (in which case it is no longer perfect). As with the scholastic doctrine of omnipotence, there is a sense in which the affirmation of God's changelessness is surely true. God is not fickle. God is not capricious. God does not have an unstable character. But the biblical understanding of God's "change-lessness" is something entirely positive. God is completely steadfast and faithful in character and purpose. It is this constancy and faith-fulness of God that the psalmist praises. It is also what the author of Hebrews has in mind in declaring that "Jesus Christ is the same yesterday and today and forever" (Heb. 13:8). We can count on God because God is faithful.

Precisely because God is faithful, we need to say that in some respects God does change. God does different things and experiences new things in interaction with the world. Just as we may engage in different activities as we pursue a single goal, so God does new things for the salvation of the world while remaining the same in character and purpose. Nowhere is the failure of theology to correct its philo-sophical inheritance in the light of the biblical story more evident than in the doctrine of the immutability of God. Whereas Scripture affirms that God has a purpose and remains faithful to that purpose precisely by doing new and surprising things, scholastic theology gets bogged down in the argument that God is immutable in every respect. The idea of God as absolutely unchanging is bought at a great price. Absolute immutability is a definition of death. An idea or principle does not move. A corpse does not move. But the living God moves and acts. In Jesus Christ we see the perfect, steadfast love of the liv-ing God, not the immutability of a dead abstraction.

A third important attribute of God in scholastic theology is *impas-sibility*. This can have two closely related meanings. It can mean God is passionless, and it can also mean God is free from all suffering. If God is impassible in the first sense, God's own being is devoid of all affect, all feeling or emotion. If God is impassible in the second sense, God may act on the creation but what happens in the creation has no impact on God. God is absolutely self-sufficient, entirely independent of others. The impassive God cannot experience need or weakness. In short, God is totally invulnerable. Once again, the intent of these affir-mations is to praise God in the highest terms possible. God is not a slave of unruly impulses. God does not have evil passions as do the scheming and adulterous ancient Greek gods of Mount Olympus. Nevertheless, while intending to offer an exalted way of speaking of God, the description of God as passionless collides head on with the biblical witness. Is God's love devoid of passion? Does not the God of the Bible have a passion for justice? Does not God respond to the cries of the suffering and the afflicted with compassion? Is God not affected by prayers of both praise and lamentation? Has not God in Jesus Christ "so loved the world that he gave his only Son" (John 3:16)? Did not Christ weep over Jerusalem? Did he not suffer the consequences of human sin for the salvation of the world? In the light of the gospel story, we must say that God, far from being impassible, is passionate, suffering love. If God is love as demonstrated in Jesus' love for us, then receptivity, vulnerability, and suffering are not strange to God's being. God is free to love more deeply than we can imagine, free to take the suffering and brokenness of the world into the very life of God and provide healing there.

The discussion of the attributes of God in scholastic theology seems at first majestic and impressive. But the resulting image of God is cold and distant. It is a picture of God far inferior to the God whose perfections are made known supremely in Jesus Christ. When we compare the scholastic way of describing what God is like with the biblical witness, we experience the great tension that made Pascal declare: "God of Abraham, God of Isaac, God of Jacob, not of the philosophers and scholars. . . . God of Jesus Christ."

## Theology and the Exercise of Power in the Church

The influence of the classical metaphysical idea of God—as absolute, omnipotent, immutable, impassible—has been enormous. It would be a mistake, however, to place all the blame for the eclipse of the biblical understanding of the power of God on the failure of scholastic theology to be more critical in its use of the classical philosophical heritage. This explanation would be much too simplistic. We cannot ignore other factors.

As I emphasized earlier, theology and the life of faith are always related to the social, economic, and political realities of their time.

These realities do not necessarily determine theology, but they definitely influence it. We must therefore ask: Whose interests does a particular theology serve and what way of life does it support?

In the early church concern for the weak, the powerless, and the poor was paramount. Jesus preached good news to the poor and the outcast. He said that giving food to the hungry, water to the thirsty, and welcoming the stranger was doing those things to him (Matt. 25:31ff.). His ministry brought sight to the blind and release to those in the captivity of sin, guilt, and shame. What he said and did shook the worlds of the religious and political authorities. The apostle Paul also saw a deep connection between the gospel he proclaimed and a sense of solidarity with the poor. He reminded his Gentile congregation at Corinth that the Lord had become poor for their sake and urged them to gather a collection for poor Christians in Jerusalem (2 Cor. 8–9).

The movement of the church and the gospel message into the Greco-Roman world occasioned more than a recasting of the church's language. As it grew, the church required organization and administration, and this necessarily meant exercise and distribution of power. How would power be understood and how would it be used? In the fourth century, Christianity was recognized as the official religion of the Roman Empire under Constantine. This was an event of enormous significance. Church and theology were necessarily greatly influenced by their new status and new context. There were new opportunities but also new temptations. It would be easy enough to say that the church should simply have washed its hands of assuming any responsibility for the political order. But as the missiologist Lesslie Newbigin asks, would that have been faithful to the purposes of God?[6] Should the church, once persecuted by the state and now faced with the opportunity of influencing the state in the direction of the teachings of Christ, have simply declined that opportunity and retreated into its own world?

However one answers these questions, what is beyond dispute is that the church and its theology in the world of Christendom established under Constantine were now sorely tempted to understand their message and mission in ways that adjusted to their new status. This shift is reflected in the history of Christian art. In earliest Christian art the incarnate Lord is represented as a shepherd who cares for his sheep. Portraying God as a shepherd is an image of gentle strength and tender care for the weak. This way of depicting God's strong love stands in sharp contrast to any understanding of God as sheer almightiness. God's power is caring, saving power. In later Christian art, however, the shepherd image is replaced by the image of the heavenly monarch surrounded by all the symbols of imperial wealth and autocratic power. God is now the heavenly Caesar, wearing a crown of gold and surrounded by many court servants. Since the time of Constantine, the power of God has all too often been understood by both believers and unbelievers as the heavenly counterpart of the power exercised by masters, kings, and Caesars on earth. When God is pictured as a celestial Caesar, it is all too clear whose interests are being served.

Throughout the history of the church the question of power has been debated. Must Christians also employ power? Can they simply refuse to have anything to do with it? If not, what sort of power is proper to the Christian understanding of God, and what implications does this have for church life? Bishop Stephen Sykes argues persuasively that in the history of the church, there have been two basic ways of answering these questions. One has been to accept power structures in the life of the church as necessary and potentially beneficial. The other has been to reject hierarchical structures in the church as incompatible with the gospel.[7] Augustine and Calvin are theologians who accept the need of law, discipline, and institutional offices for the well-being of the church. John Yoder and Jürgen Moltmann are theologians who reject hierarchy and decision making by a few in the life of the church and seek to replace it with communal life characterized by "dialogue, consensus and harmony."[8]

The practices of the church and the way the church organizes its common life say at least as much to the world around it as does its verbal witness. According to Karl Barth, the life and order of the church, as well as its proclamation, should be both a reminder and a promise, "that there is already on earth a community whose order is based on that great alteration of the human situation" that has occurred in God's work of reconciliation in Jesus Christ.[9] In other words, whatever the order of the church, it should be exemplary of the kind of life in community that the gospel seeks to foster. The church in its life as well as in its proclamation is called to be a witness to the reign of God. While it is far from identical with that reign, the church is called to be a provisional yet concrete sign of its coming.

What would the exercise of power look like in a church reformed and renewed in the light of the power of God made known in the crucified and risen Christ?

First, it would be a church of *participants* rather than a church made up of passive observers. It would be a church in which all would be recognized as recipients of the life-giving power of God's Word and Spirit rather than a community in which power is held and exercised only by a few. Because the Spirit gives gifts to all members of the community that are for the good of the whole, any sharp division between clergy and laity would be erased.

Second, it would be a church in which *leadership* would be a matter of service rather than prerogative. Leadership would not be defined primarily in a juridical fashion, as power over others, but in pastoral terms, as callings to serve Christ and his people by ministries of guidance and restoration. "The rulers of the Gentiles lord it over them. . . . It will not be so among you; but whoever wishes to be great among you must be your servant" (Matt. 20:25–26).

Third, it would be a church whose *mission* was centered not on itself but on God's coming reign inaugurated in the ministry, death, and resurrection of Christ. It would be a church that resisted making pretentious claims about itself and that found its joy and its vocation in the grace and promise of God in Jesus Christ that is to be proclaimed to all people. It would be a church concerned for the poor and the outcast and an advocate of justice and peace.

Fourth, it would be a church that knew it was called to deal differently and *noncoercively* with the issues of the exercise of power in community. It would be, in short, a church where tensions and conflicts over the exercise of power are resolved prayerfully, in open discussion, and in conformity with the Spirit of Christ, and not by recourse to the civil courts.

A theology that loses touch with the gospel of the crucified Lord will fail to challenge the common life and everyday practices of the church. We must therefore dare to question prevailing views of the power of God and their implications for church life.

How do the decisions and practices of the local church reflect its understanding of the *omnipotence* of God? Whose interests are served by the sermons we preach or hear, the church budgets we vote on, the church school programs we design, the way the church recognizes leadership, organizes itself, and uses its power? How does the everyday government of our churches reflect our view of the power of God whom we worship? Do we equate power with the kind of control and mastery over others that characterizes the power plays of secular institutions? Is this the de facto understanding of power that lies behind the way our denomination or our local church is governed? Do we assume that power in the church should be concentrated in one person or in one central committee? Is the organization of our church a witness to the diversity of the gifts of the Spirit, to the fact that all the people of God are bearers of the Spirit's gifts, and not just a select few? Do we think that men have the exclusive power and right to exercise authority over women? What sort of witness does the church's form of government make to the larger human community about the proper nature, fruitful distribution, and responsible exercise of power?

Let me be clear. There are many forms of church governance, and none can be said to be perfect. Episcopal, synodical, and congregational forms of church order all have their strengths and weaknesses. None can claim to be the sole heir of the biblical witness. Each can make a strong case for its special aptness to meet the need of particular times and circumstances.

What is beyond dispute, however, is that the church cannot be considered a "power-free zone."[10] Some form of order and leadership is necessary in every community, including the community called the church. It is sheer romanticism to think it can be otherwise. A responsible alternative to the abuse of power either in church or in society is not the rejection of all exercise of power. Declaring that we must either resign ourselves to the abuse of power even in the life of the church, or simply refuse as Christians to have anything to do with the use of power, is a false alternative. The real question for the church is how does the different power of God that is supremely manifest in Jesus Christ transform our understanding and exercise of power?

The church must continually test not only its forms of organization but also its ways of evangelization. How do our methods of evangelism express our understanding of the power of God? Do we employ a hard-sell technique? Are we openly or subtly coercive in our efforts to communicate the gospel? Do we respect the traditions and cultural heritages of other people? Do we measure our "success" as a church simply by membership rolls and budget figures?

If a rethinking of God's omnipotence in the light of the gospel mandates an examination of appropriate order and use of power in the church, we must also dare to question the idea of divine *immutability* as it bears on the life of the church. What are we trying to say when we call God immutable or unchangeable? If we think of God as immutable in every sense, how does this affect our attitudes toward change in the church and in society? Are we afraid of change? Do we think life would be fine if nothing ever changed? Do we long for the old-time religion when what was right and what was wrong were absolutely clear (or so we suppose)? Do we want a church where doctrines and ethical teachings are not subject to examination and must remain as absolutely immutable as we suppose God to be? Do we really believe and trust in the *living* God? If we insist on immutability in the life of the church, what witness do we bear to the larger society in which we live? Do we favor an immobile society, one in which everyone stays in his or her God-given place? Do we resent or even resist efforts on the part of people who are working for change in our society in the direction of greater justice and freedom for those now deprived and exploited?

Finally, we must dare to question the idea of God's *impassibility*, or inability to suffer, and speak boldly of the passion and suffering of God, and we must ask what the implications of this might be for the life and mission of the church. What do we mean when we call God impassible? Do we want an invulnerable God because we secretly crave invulnerability to the suffering and affliction of the world? Do we want a passionless God because we are afraid of our own passions or because we are disturbed by the passion of others for justice, freedom, and human wholeness? Does our belief in God set us in opposition to conditions of oppression and injustice, to evils like racism and sexism, or does our belief in God, whom we call impassible, make us indifferent to these evils? Does our faith in God prepare us to face real conflicts in personal relationships and in society, or does it obscure or ignore these conflicts for the sake of peace at any price? Does our understanding of God encourage us to be advocates of the health and well-being of all people? Does our understanding of God have anything to do with such things as universal health care and immigration policies? The prophet Micah asks, "What does the LORD require of you but to do justice, and to love kindness, and to walk humbly with your God?" (Mic. 6:8). Does our understanding of God's passion for justice fill us with the passion for new life in a transformed world?

These are difficult and disturbing questions. Yet if we claim to be disciples of Christ, we must have the courage to ask them. The pilgrimage of faith requires honest examination of our understandings of God in the light of the gospel. It involves asking whose interests our understandings of God and the church are serving and what way of life they are supporting.

The church exists not for itself but for the world. But the church obscures its service to the world if its own form of life is only a small replica of the bureaucracy and subtle coercion that characterize the use of power in the surrounding society rather than offering a hopeful sign of a truly different exercise of power in human community.

## The Power of God the Creator, Redeemer, and Transformer

If descriptions of God as omnipotent, immutable, and impassible are misleading unless redefined by the gospel, the remedy is not to speak of God as ineffective, inconsistent, and sentimental. This has been the mistake of some modern theologies in their attempt to get beyond scholastic ways of thinking. Whereas the tendency of scholastic theology is to exalt the power of God at the expense of divine compassion, the tendency of some modern theology is to exalt the compassion of God at the expense of God's power and justice. All of our images of God must be radically revised in the light of Jesus Christ the crucified and risen Lord. He is the central clue, the key that unlocks the right understanding of authentic divine power and fruitful human power. Martin Luther King Jr. had the standard of Jesus Christ in mind when he said: "Power without love is reckless and abusive, and love without power is sentimental and anemic. Power at its best is love implementing the demands of justice."[11]

If we describe the attributes of God on the basis of what we think God should be like, the result will be arbitrary. What we call God will be only our secret fears and sinful desires. A description of the attributes of God, if it is faithful to the biblical witness, will focus on God's covenantal love for Israel and decisively on what God does and suffers for the world in Jesus Christ. No theologian of the modern period has adhered to this principle more consistently than Karl Barth:

> We may believe that God can and must only be absolute in contrast to all that is relative, exalted in contrast to all that is lowly, active in contrast to all suffering, inviolable in contrast to all temptation, transcendent in contrast to all immanence, and therefore divine in contrast to everything human, in short that He can and must be only the "Wholly Other." But such beliefs are shown to be quite untenable, and corrupt and pagan, by the fact that God does in fact be and do this in Jesus Christ.[12]

Note the central point of what Barth says in this passage. God can be and is a lowly, suffering, fully human being in Jesus Christ. Yet God becomes one of us in Jesus Christ *without ceasing to be God*. If we attend to the New Testament witness, we will not be content to speak of the power of God in abstract or vague terms. The gospel story redefines the power of God. It is the power of God at work decisively in Christ and in his Spirit. It is what God the Father does in giving his Son for the salvation of the world. It is what the Son of God does in graciously reaching out to include the sinful and the poor in God's kingdom and finally in giving his life on the cross to reconcile all things to God. It is what the Spirit of God does to enliven and transform all who trust in him. God is creator, redeemer, and transformer of life—not mere almightiness but creative power; not impassive but compassionate power; not immutable but steadfast, life-giving power that liberates and transforms the world.

We confess God as our *creator*. The idea of the creation of the world conjures up the thought of an enormous exercise of power. Can we even begin to imagine the power released in the creation of the universe? Our universe with all its galaxies and countless stars had its origin in a powerful event of unimaginable dimensions. In contrast to such unthinkable power, whatever power human beings possess seems puny and insignificant. All creatures are radically dependent on the stupendous power of their creator. Thinking about God the Creator in this way has its benefits. It may lead us to praise of our Creator and to an honest recognition of our human limits. It may contribute to a spirit of humility. But there are also possibilities of serious misunderstanding in this way of thinking. For the primary mark of God's power is not sheer omnipotence but goodness and beneficence. Far from being a mighty explosion of aimless power, the power of God the Creator is purposeful and life-giving.

One of the most remarkable features of the Genesis creation stories is that God does not create the world in an act of violence. Other ancient creation stories, such as the Babylonian *Enuma elish,* speak about God's slaying a dragon or engaging in other acts of violence in order to create the world. But the God of the biblical witness simply speaks a nonviolent word to bring the world into being: "Then God said, 'Let there be light'; and there was light" (Gen. 1:3). Creation is not an act of violence but sheer gift.

What we learn from God's work as creator is that truly creative power always involves discipline and self-restraint on the part of the creator. This is evident in good parenting. It is also present in the work of every artist. A sculptor respects the qualities of the material he shapes. A painter honors the nature of colors and textures. A novelist allows the characters in her novel to have their own personality and independence. These are, of course, only faint analogies of the creative power of God. The power of God is different. In creating the world, God gives existence to what previously did not exist. God the Creator does not begrudge existence to another. God gives his creatures the power to be and to love. The power of God the Creator is empowering power. According to the Genesis story of creation, God gives human beings a share in the dominion over the earth. Creation has a purpose. It is not a whimsical display of almightiness or the result of the sheer self-assertiveness of deity. As an act of letting another exist and of sharing life with this other, creation is an act of love and, like all love, involves self-limitation. Understanding the act of creation in this way enables us to see both creation and redemption as acts of grace. The cross and resurrection of Jesus Christ are the climactic expression of God's creative power. The power of the Creator, like the power of the Redeemer, is the altogether different power of omnipotent love.

We confess God as our *redeemer*. In Jesus Christ we know God as compassionate power. God is not indifferent to creation and its destiny. God cares passionately for the world. Unlike the God of deism, the God of the biblical witness does not remain aloof toward and unaffected by the sin and suffering of creatures. God freely creates the world and freely suffers for the sake of its redemption. This compassionate power of God is perfectly embodied in the person and work of Jesus Christ. As revealed in Christ, God's compassion is not mere powerlessness any more than God's act of creation is sheer almightiness. God's compassion shows itself to be stronger than sin and death. Weak if measured by the standard of compulsion, the compassionate power of God revealed in the cross of Christ is "the power for salvation," strong to save a world in bondage to self-centeredness, compulsion, and violence. From the sickness of seeking mastery and control over others, God can save us only by the exercise of a wholly different kind of power—the power of suffering love.

We confess God as our *renewer.* In the power of the Spirit, the giver of new life, the crucified One is raised. In the power of the Spirit, we are transformed into the image of our creator and redeemer. The power of the Spirit is not bombastic, sensational, show-off power. It is not self-aggrandizing power. Such power would only be a repetition of what is offered by the principalities and powers of the world. It would not be renewing and transforming. It would not liberate us from the various bondages we experience. The power of the Spirit unites us to the gracious, self-limiting, and other-regarding power of our Creator and Redeemer. To speak of the power of God the Holy Spirit as immutable would be grotesque. Immutable means motionless; the Spirit is in constant motion to further human transformation and to bring the whole creation to completion in God's kingdom of justice and peace. Immutable means lifeless; the Spirit is the power of new life. Immutable means changeless; the Spirit is the power of repentance, conversion, and new beginning, the power that changes everything.

Christians do not sing praises to the absolute of the philosophers. They sing, "All hail the power of Jesus' name!" Christians do not proclaim the story of Superman or Superwoman. They tell the story of Jesus, the Suffering Servant, whose power is entirely different from the principalities and powers of a world in bondage. Christians do not pray and baptize in the name of the omnipotent, the immutable, the impassible. They pray and baptize in the name of the Father, the Son, and the Holy Spirit, and to this living God they sing:

> Praise God, the Source of life and birth,
> Praise God, the Word enfleshed on earth,
> Praise God, the Spirit, Holy Flame,
> All glory, honor to God's name!

## Questions for Discussion

1. How might the practices of a local Christian congregation and the way it organizes itself reflect its understanding of the power of God?
2. In what ways does God remain ever the same, and in what ways does God change? Are there teachings and practices of the church that should remain the same, and are there others that should be open to change?
3. If we say that God suffers, does that mean that God is a tragic victim like so many others, and is unable to conquer sin, suffering, and death?

5

# The Power of God Who Freely Loves

*As you, Father, are in me and I am in you, may they also be in us*
(John 17:21)

## The Meaning of the Doctrine of the Trinity

For many Christians the doctrine of the Trinity is the most obscure and confusing teaching of the church. The talk of God as "three persons in one essence" seems to defy logic and common sense. Of all Christian teachings about God, this one seems to be the least illuminating and the least significant for everyday Christian faith and practice. This is a feeling shared not only by laypeople but by many clergy as well. The story is told of a pastor who faced the task of preaching on Trinity Sunday with much misgiving. He solved his problem by informing his congregation that the Trinity was such a great mystery that in honor of it there would be no sermon that morning!

Despite widespread confusion about its meaning, the doctrine of the Trinity represents the distinctively Christian understanding of God. The Trinitarian understanding of God is deeply etched in Christian prayer and worship. We baptize in the name of the triune God (Matt. 28:19). We bless in the name of the triune God (2 Cor. 13:13). We sing praises to the triune God:

> Holy, holy, holy!
> merciful and mighty!
> God in three Persons,
> blessed Trinity!

The doctrine of the Trinity is indelibly stamped not only on Christian hymns and prayers but also on the classical creeds and confessions of the church. In a very real sense, the doctrine of the Trinity is a summary of the Christian gospel. In this chapter, I will try to explain why Trinitarian doctrine is crucial for a Christian understanding of the power of God.

In the two previous chapters I have already indicated that the New Testament witness to the reality and power of God is implicitly Trinitarian. Jesus Christ, his ministry, death, and resurrection, is clearly the center of the New Testament message. Yet the person and work of Jesus cannot be rightly understood apart from his relationship to God the Father on the one hand and his relationship to the Spirit of God on the other. As God's beloved Son, Jesus loves and freely obeys the Father who sent him on his redemptive mission. Moreover, Jesus both uniquely bears God's Spirit and sends the Spirit from the Father to the disciples to empower their ministry in his name. The gospel story in its fullness can be told only in Trinitarian terms. God the Father so loved the world that he gave his only Son to redeem it (John 3:16); Jesus Christ the Son of God freely emptied himself and became a humble servant for our salvation even to the abyss of death on a cross (Phil. 2:5ff.); the Spirit of resurrection power (Rom. 8:11) who comes from the Father and the Son moves freely in the world to transform and direct it toward God's new world of justice and peace.

Thus the doctrine of the Trinity, often maligned and misunderstood, is not the result of murky thinking or the product of ecclesiastical smoke and mirrors. It is simply the effort of the church—in language that is true but inevitably inadequate—to affirm what God is really like in the light of God's unique presence in Jesus the crucified and risen Lord and in the coming of the Holy Spirit. We do not engage in wild speculation when we call God triune. On the contrary, we simply confess that God has been revealed to us in this way—as a Trinity of self-giving, other-affirming, community-forming love.

While a Trinitarian understanding of God is implicit in the New Testament witness, the full development of the doctrine took several centuries. A crucial issue involved in the development of the doctrine of the Trinity is the question of the nature of God's power. Is the kind of power at work in Jesus the ultimate power of God? Or is the power of God the

Father different from and greater than what is seen in Jesus the cruci- fied and risen Lord? At the Council of Nicaea in AD 325 the church declared that Jesus Christ is of "one substance" with the Father. This affirmation was directed against a priest named Arius, who wanted to reserve real divinity—ultimate power—to God the Father. Arius's Jesus was divine but not fully God, not God in the same sense that the Father Almighty was God. The church rightly decided against Arius that to separate the ultimate power of God from Jesus would be to create an idol of the human imagination—the idea of sheer almightiness untainted by the scandal of the cross. This would separate ultimate power and redemptive power. It would declare that there is in fact another God, a hidden God, a God behind the back, as it were, of the God revealed in Jesus Christ. When the church declared that Jesus Christ is of "one sub- stance" with the Father, it reaffirmed its trust in Jesus who said: "Who- ever has seen me has seen the Father" (John 14:9).

If the Son embodies the true power of God in human form, the Holy Spirit re-presents this power in all space and time. Thus at the Coun- cil of Constantinople in AD 381 the church confessed the co-divinity of the Holy Spirit, together with the Father and the Son. The Spirit is "the Lord, the Giver of Life . . . who with the Father and the Son is worshiped and glorified." The liberating and reconciling power of the Spirit is one with the power of the Father and the Son.

The doctrine of the Trinity represents a revolution in the under- standing of the power of God. It is a revolution in faith and theology far more momentous than the Copernican revolution in astronomy, the Einsteinian revolution in physics, or the American and French revo- lutions in politics. Christians do not worship absolute power. They worship God, whose different power is described in the gospel story and symbolized in the doctrine of the Trinity. The power of God is shared power, transforming power, power that makes for just and inclusive community. Here is a radically new beginning in our under- standing of God and especially of God's power. Every previous idea of divinity and every previous understanding of human power must be thoroughly and continuously revised in the light of the supreme power of the triune God.

When Christians confess their faith, using the Apostles' Creed or the Nicene Creed (the most widely used creeds of the church), they affirm a Trinitarian faith in "God the Father Almighty," in "Jesus Christ his only Son our Lord," and in "the Holy Spirit, the Lord and Giver of life." According to Trinitarian faith, God is not a vague "God in general." The triune God is *this* God: not just any sort of power or creativity and certainly not raw, arbitrary power; but "God the Father Almighty"; Creator of heaven and earth; not just any power that claims to be able to save us but Jesus Christ, God's "only Son," our crucified and risen Lord; not just any power claimed to offer spiritual vitality or religious ecstasy but God's Holy Spirit, "the Lord and Giver of Life" who comes from the loving Father and the loving Son, and who liberates and transforms us here and now. Trinitarian faith is startlingly specific in its description of the one who is confessed as God.

During the past fifty years or so, the doctrine of the Trinity has moved once again to the center of Christian theological discussion.[1] The central importance of this often neglected doctrine for Christian faith and life has been reclaimed by theologians of all denominations (Karl Barth, Karl Rahner, Jürgen Moltmann, Hans Urs von Balthasar, Elizabeth Johnson, and John Zizioulas, among others). They have argued that, far from being the product of mere speculation, the doctrine of the Trinity points to a great mystery at the heart of Christian faith. Christians think and speak of God as Trinity not out of an urge to speculate but out of faithfulness to the whole gospel story of Jesus the crucified and risen Lord. While we can never exhaust the mystery of the Trinity, when we call God triune we are pointing to several truths about the eternal reality of God.[2]

First, the doctrine of the Trinity affirms that the one God who created the heavens and the earth cannot be separated from the crucified and risen Jesus or from his renewing Spirit. According to the New Testament witness, we know God as the Father who loves and sends the Son; as the Son who loves and obeys the Father; as the Spirit who is sent by the Father and the Son to draw us into their relationship. The one God is the faithful Father, the servant Son, and the enlivening Spirit. Christians confess that *God is alive and personal in these three ways*. Trinitarian doctrine declares that these different ways in which God has related to us are not accidental but rooted in the eternal being of God. God is not a lifeless thing or a solitary entity; God acts and abides in personal relationships, not only in his relationship to his creatures but in God's own being in all eternity. The triune God does not first become loving or first attain to personhood by relating to the world. God is eternally love, and love means being with and for another. In the richness of the eternal triune life of love there are personal distinctions. The inner dynamism of the triune life makes room for difference. If we have a superficial or sentimental view of love, we are prone to think that it is threatened or even destroyed by differences. The love of the triune God, however, is strong and deep enough to affirm and celebrate real differences not only in God's relationship to the world and among the manifold creatures of God but also in God's own life. Fear of differences among our fellow creatures— whether racial, sexual, or cultural—may finally betray an understanding of God as utterly monotonous. The Trinitarian vision of God stands in contrast to the destructive anxiety that drives us to reduce all personal, social, and political existence to a deadening uniformity, as happens in totalitarian movements such as Nazism and Stalinism or in social and political programs of apartheid and ethnic cleansing.

Second, the doctrine of the Trinity declares that *God's own life is communal* or social in nature. The life of God is not dead uniformity. God is not mere mathematical oneness. There are differences within the living unity of God. God does not affirm difference merely for its own sake. God affirms distinct persons in relationship for the sake of community, for the sake of friendship and mutual love. Friendship and love are given and received by those who are different, yet whose love binds them together without dissolving their differences. According to Trinitarian doctrine, God is not the will to power but the will to communion in freedom. God is not absolute force that crushes all opposition but the power of peaceful coexistence, the will to be with and for others, the spirit of solidarity that creates and sustains life in just and fruitful relationships. Community arises when persons are in free, reciprocal, affirming relationships with one another. On the one hand, we can never be persons in total solitude and absolute independence but only in relationship and community. On the other hand, real community exists only as persons are respected and loved in their particularity and distinctiveness rather than being required to conform to some abstract principle of unity. As Father, Son, and Spirit, God exists in communion and is the source of true community. The communion of the triune God, of course, is far deeper than anything we may experience in our relationships with others. God exists as three persons profoundly united in mutually indwelling love. The Trinitarian theological tradition has spoken of this unique union of the triune persons by the technical term *perichoresis,* a communion in self-giving love so deep that each of the persons is inseparably bound to the others. Each "permeates," "exists in," and "indwells" the others.

Third, the mystery of the Trinity means that *God is the power of self-giving love*. This is the deepest meaning of God's triune life-in-relationship. This is what decisively marks off the living God from the dead idols. They cannot give life because they cannot love. They cannot love because they cannot enter into communion with and freely suffer for another. The true God is alive and gives life to others. This is an understanding of God centered on the crucified and risen Christ and the work of his Spirit. God is not turned in upon Godself. In Word and Spirit God goes forth to another in love. As self-communicating love, God is open to suffering for the sake of the beloved. From all eternity God is defined by this self-giving action, by this movement of Word and Spirit. For this reason it is necessary to say that in the eternal life of God there is a readiness for the creation of the world and for the incarnation and suffering of Jesus Christ for the world's salvation. The coming of the Son of God and his sacrificial death on the cross are neither chance happenings nor emergency measures nor out-of-character actions on God's part. The self-giving love of God for the world embodied in Christ and communicated to us by the Spirit is grounded in God's eternal triune being. From eternity the triune God is the God who freely loves in himself and freely determines to be God for us. In creating and redeeming the world, the eternal love of God, eternally shared in the triune life, is freely extended outward. God's liberating and reconciling activity in the world is the free outward expression of God's own eternal life of self-giving love. God did not have to create or redeem this world. These are free acts of love. In neither case was God motivated to act from some factor outside God or from some deficiency in God. Yet in acting on our behalf, God is true to Godself. The life of the triune God is in the communion of love, and God invites our participation in this communion. As Jesus prayed, "As you, Father, are in me and I am in you, may they also be in us"

(John 17:21). The triune God is eternally open for costly relationship with the world, for God is love (1 John 4:8).

## The Trinity and Human Suffering

If the Trinity is the deepest mystery of God, the immensity of suffering in the world—especially the suffering of the innocent—is the greatest mystery of human life. Unless we can see a relationship between these two mysteries, faith in God will always appear abstract and removed from life. As long as God is imagined as the absolute— omnipotent, immutable, impassible—no connection can be seen between the mystery of God and the mystery of human suffering. Such a God, however, is not the God proclaimed as Father, Son, and Holy Spirit in the gospel and in the worship of the church.

The mystery of suffering and evil is familiar to the biblical witnesses and to believers of every age. Why does God allow so much suffering in the world? Why did God allow millions of Africans to be traded into slavery, either to die in the great passage, or to live out their lives in immeasurable pain of body and spirit? Why did God allow Nazi executioners to machine-gun their helpless victims or murder them in gas chambers? Why does God allow innocent children to die of hunger? Why does God allow the destruction of innocents by nuclear weapons and suicide bombers? Why hurricanes like Katrina? Why tsunamis that kill a quarter of a million people?

Contemporary writers are haunted by these questions. In the novel *Sophie's Choice*, William Styron describes the horrible experience of Sophie, a Polish Catholic mother of two young children, upon their entering the concentration camp at Auschwitz. A Nazi commandant orders the mother to choose which child she will keep and which will be sent to the gas chamber. It is an unspeakably diabolical choice. Forced to choose in order to save one child, Sophie loses her faith in God and very nearly her sanity. The commandant, we are told, considered the choice he offered quite generous; after all, he had the power to take both children.[3]

Another narrative of profound human suffering is Toni Morrison's novel *The Beloved*. Set in 1873, it tells the story of Sethe, a black woman who eighteen years earlier had escaped from slavery with her children. Tracked down by her hunters who came to take her and her children back to their owner, Sethe had done the only thing she could to prevent the hunters from taking her children back to a hellish life worse than death. Before she could be stopped, she had slain her little girl, named Beloved, rather than allow her to be returned to the loveless and hopeless world of slavery. Years later, struggling to find consolation and meaning, Sethe is haunted by the ghost of her Beloved and the memory of the terrible deed that had been driven by a mother's deep and desperate love.[4]

The horrors of slavery, genocides, concentration camps, and other atrocities of modern warfare have made it not only intellectually difficult but also morally reprehensible to believe in the omnipotent God of much traditional theology. What shall we say if God is able to stop all the carnage of history and refuses to do so? Is God then a monster? In Robert Browning's poem *Pippa Passes*, Pippa sings,

> God's in his heaven—
> All's right with the world!

After the glow and stench of the ovens at Auschwitz, the cruelties of slavery, the barbarities of torture and suicide bombings, the countless children who die of disease or starvation in the poorest nations of the world, a confession of faith like Pippa's no longer seems believable or even honest. Many persons, both inside and outside the church, would now find much more convincing the hard choice posed by Satan in Archibald MacLeish's play *J.B.*:

> If God is God, he is not good.
> If God is good, he is not God.
> Take the even, take the odd.[5]

Numerous attempts have been made by theologians to defend God's goodness in the face of the reality of suffering and evil (an effort called theodicy). One such attempt declares that the evil that human beings experience is entirely the result of the misuse of human freedom. If men and women are to be free agents rather than mere puppets, God must permit evil events to happen. Suffering is the unavoidable result of the creation of a world in which human beings have the capacity to turn away from God and do harm to their fellow creatures. According to another argument, suffering is to be interpreted as a form of divine judgment and as a stern call to repentance and a new way of life. Still another argument is that suffering and evil can be put to a good use. They provide occasion for spiritual growth that would not otherwise be possible.

Such answers to the mystery of suffering and evil may possess a grain of truth. In the Bible there are examples of all of these approaches to suffering. Most of us can think of particular instances in our own experience when one or another of these responses might have been appropriate and might have offered some consolation. But none of these proposals goes to the heart of the biblical witness concerning God and human suffering. They fail to focus on the transformation of the meaning of the power of God by the gospel of God's presence in the suffering, death, and resurrection of Jesus. Out of love, God freely suffers for the salvation of others—that is the deepest message of Scripture regarding human suffering.

Dietrich Bonhoeffer was a young theologian martyred by the Nazis. In a famous and provocative note written in his prison cell, he declared: "Only a suffering God can help."[6] Only a God who knows the suffering and affliction of the human race to the utmost limits can help us. Only such a God can liberate us from our monstrous corruption of power, can reconcile us to God and to our fellow creatures, can promise new life in the midst of death.

Adolfo Pérez Esquivel, an Argentine Roman Catholic artist, winner of the Nobel Peace Prize, and leader of an ecumenical group that works with the poor of Latin America, offers a contemporary image of the suffering God in a painting entitled *Christ of the Poncho*. The artist depicts Christ in a poncho, the garment that is worn by peasants when the cold descends on the Andes or the rains deluge the tropical forests. The suffering God is present wherever there is affliction or need.

The suffering God is the triune God. Only the Trinitarian understanding of God consistently and unambiguously affirms that God, the Creator and Lord of all, experiences the deepest abyss of human suffering, abandonment, and death for the sake of our salvation. The doctrine of the Trinity expresses what we know of God in the light of the crucified Jesus who was raised to new life in the power of the Spirit.

On the cross, Jesus cries, "My God, my God, why have you forsaken me?" (Mark 15:34). Jesus cries on behalf of all humanity and all creation. But his cry is also the cry of God, who in his Son goes to the depths of human brokenness and suffering and makes it his own. The passion and death of Jesus are not God's punishment, anger, or revenge directed at an innocent human victim. Nor is this cry of Jesus an indication of his loss of faith and trust in his Father. On the contrary, the crucified Jesus is the unsurpassable embodiment of the triune God's costly love for the world. All of the world's pain and suffering are taken into the life of God on the cross. In the incarnation and its culmination in the crucifixion, God the Father gives his Son to the world out of love. In obedience to the Father's will, Jesus freely gives himself for our salvation, even to death on a cross. With Psalm 22 on his lips, he continues to trust in God even as he experiences the loneliness and agony of crucifixion. Father and Son are bound together by the Spirit of this costly love for the world, and the Spirit radiates this love throughout the creation. The Spirit moves us to repentance and faith, creates in us a new freedom and joy, incites us to pray, encourages us to resist evil powers and to give ourselves in service to God's coming reign of justice, freedom, and peace throughout the creation.

The doctrine of the Trinity does not give us a theodicy. It does not attempt to explain the presence of evil in a world created good by God. Instead it tells us what God is doing to overcome evil in the world. It affirms the faithfulness of God to the world despite the reality of sin and misery. In the light of the gospel story, we know that the triune God is the God of suffering love who takes the sin, suffering, and violence of the world into the very heart of God. God is the Father who sends his Son and grieves over his loss; God is the Son who as one of us and on our behalf cries out in affliction on the cross; God is the Spirit who groans with the entire suffering creation as he works for the coming of the glorious liberty of the children of God (Rom. 8:21–23).[7]

Does this reduce God to a helpless and pitiful deity? Far from it, and for two reasons. First, the triune God *freely* suffers for the world in bondage to sin and death. God *willingly* shares our misery and bears the judgment we deserve in order to bring forgiveness, freedom, and new life. The God who is able and willing to suffer with and for us all is not a mere victim of fate or necessity but the sovereign Lord of the universe. When God in Christ "emptied himself" (Phil. 2:5ff.) and became a suffering servant for our sake, this was an act both of God's free grace and of God's relentless judgment on all human pride, cruelty, and injustice.

Second, the gospel of God's self-giving love does not end in unrelieved tragedy and hopelessness. On the contrary, the good news is that God's suffering love is victorious. This is the meaning of the confession, Jesus Christ the crucified is risen! In Christ, God is victor as well as victim. The love of God is not pitiful and ineffectual but singularly powerful. If the victory of the love of God is not yet evident to all, the resurrection of Christ and the working of his Spirit are God's promise of final and universal victory. Jesus' resurrection from the dead is God's own verdict on what Jesus has done for the salvation of the world. It is also the promise of the ultimate triumph of the costly grace of God. God's victory over sin and suffering is won not by force but by God's self-giving love that bears the full brunt of evil. Evil exhausts itself in its opposition to that which is inexhaustibly good. This is the way in which the love of God wins its victory. The Spirit of the risen Christ continues to liberate and transform human life by the different power of omnipotent, unconquerable love.

In speaking of the suffering of God and of our Christian calling to take up the cross of discipleship, do we give support to the idea that all suffering is willed by God? Not at all. The message of Christ crucified reminds us of the great difference between suffering that is inflicted on others and redemptive suffering that is freely accepted in the struggle against evil. The suffering love of God does not sanctify the abuse of power; it places all unjust and cruel exercise of power under judgment. The suffering love of God not only moves us to gratitude for mercy undeserved; it also arouses us to resist all forms of injustice and oppression.

It would be a terrible mistake to understand the doctrine of the Trinity as a mere theoretical solution to the mystery of evil and suffering. Every attempt to offer a theoretical answer to the why of suffering quickly falls into the trap of explaining it away. Suffering is not primarily a theoretical problem but an agonizing reality of life. Far from being an attempt to justify all suffering as necessary or good, the belief that God suffers with and for us speaks to questions that arise from the depths of human life: Is God completely trustworthy? Can we trust in God as our companion in suffering and death? Can we look to God as one who does not glorify suffering in itself but instead freely accompanies us in our resistance to and protest against suffering that can be averted or that human beings impose on each other? These burning questions cannot be answered affirmatively if the God we worship is limitless, impassive, coercive power. We can respond affirmatively, however, if the God we worship and adore is the triune God. God calls us to follow Jesus, to open ourselves in love to the costly risks of Christian discipleship, not because we enjoy suffering but for the sake of a more just world, a world in which people live in communion with God and in friendship and peace with one another.

## The Trinity and the Coming Reign of God

The doctrine of the Trinity proclaims the distinctive power of God in creation, redemption, and the consummation of all things. God the Three-in-One is not only the source of life, not only the power that judges and redeems life from the bondage of sin and death, but also the power that moves the world toward God's coming reign. The gift of the Spirit of Christ brings the "first fruits" (Rom. 8:23) of God's coming reign of freedom, justice, and peace. Led by the Spirit, Christians are called to work and pray for greater justice and peace on earth, but they are not to confuse these efforts with the final joy and glory of God's coming reign.

How can we best symbolize the Christian hope for the reign of God? The biblical images of the coming rule of God are numerous. It is portrayed as a time of peace and harmony in all of the creation.

> They shall beat their swords into plowshares,
>     and their spears into pruning hooks;
> nation shall not lift up sword against nation,
>     neither shall they learn war any more.
>                                         (Isa. 2:4)

> The wolf shall live with the lamb,
>     and the leopard shall lie down with the kid,

the calf and the lion and the fatling together,
and a little child shall lead them.
(Isa. 11:6)

The reign of God is also pictured as a beautiful heavenly city (Rev. 21:2), as a father's house (John 14:2), as a great feast (Matt. 8:11), as a new heaven and a new earth (Rev. 21:1). This is only a sampling of the treasury of biblical images of God's coming rule. They portray in various ways the completion of God's purposes, the total conquest of sin and death, the end of hostility and war, the realization of perfect justice and freedom, the final triumph of God over all forces that spoil the good creation.

While we are familiar with many of these images, we may not recognize Trinitarian doctrine as an incomparable image of hope, a beautiful symbol of life in perfect community. In the life of the Trinity there is an eternal giving and receiving of love. Father, Son, and Spirit are one, yet distinct; perfectly free, yet perfectly bound to each other. Here is personal identity and freedom that does not destroy community; here is community that does not demand the sacrifice of personal identity and freedom. As described in Trinitarian doctrine, God's reign is unsurpassed life in shared love, life in perfect commonwealth.

The beauty and relevance of this Trinitarian vision of final fulfillment stands out sharply when it is compared with other images of hope that struggle for the allegiance of humanity today. One is the private utopia of autonomous individuals. Happiness is sought in self-realization, in the possession of things, and in the exercise of power over other people. Modern Western society—especially North American society—promotes this dream from cradle to coffin. Our national heroes are "self-made" individuals who have "lifted themselves up by their bootstraps." We expect businesses and corporations to pursue aggressively their own growth without giving much thought to the common good. We measure the strength of individuals by their achievement of self-sufficiency and independence. In the utopia of autonomous individuals freedom and happiness are defined in terms of how much is possessed and consumed. The dream home of this utopia is a large private mansion surrounded by locked iron gates.

Despite the emptiness and loneliness it produces, the drive to "make it" by oneself and to find happiness in private wealth remains the chief hope of fulfillment for many people in modern Western society. This form of utopian thinking has no concern for a just and peaceful society that characterizes the biblical vision of the future promised by God. It elevates acquisitiveness and possessiveness over cooperation, friendship, and the cultivation of the common welfare. It confuses happiness with consumption, freedom with having many possessions, selfhood with solitary existence. However tempting it may be, the drive to possess and consume fails to satisfy our deepest human longings. We are made for community with God and with others. Fulfillment cannot be found along the path of individualism.

A second influential image of the future in our time is the utopia of collectivism built by military struggle. The hope at work in this form of utopian thinking is that through revolutionary struggle and revolutionary violence a new world will be created. After the revolution, freedom will replace bondage, justice will replace capitalistic exploitation, peace will replace class struggle. If utopia through private enterprise is the dream of millions in largely affluent societies, utopia through revolution is the dream offered to millions in the impoverished and war-torn societies of the world. In some versions of revolutionary utopia, everything and everyone must be ruthlessly subordinated to the revolutionary cause. The ends justify the means. It is not the present but the future that counts. If some people must be sacrificed now so that future generations will live in freedom, justice, and equality, the cost, however great, is justified. This is a view of future community that betrays a disregard of actual persons here and now. People are subordinated to abstract causes or principles. Let there be no mistake: the Christian gospel itself contains a revolutionary ferment; it seeks continuing transformations of social and economic life to narrow the gulf between rich and poor. The structures of the world that keep many people poor and hungry must be vigorously challenged in the name of Christ. But a new and inclusive human community cannot be built by a spirit of vengeance or a campaign of indiscriminate violence.

In *The Gulag Archipelago*, Alexander Solzhenitsyn depicts in frightening detail the systematic degradation of human beings in the labor camps of Stalinist Russia.[8] In the name of the revolution and the creation of a new social order stripped of belief in God, people suffered arbitrary arrest, the barbarian methods of the secret police, separation of family members, imprisonment without trial or appeal, and torture, exile, and death.

After the collapse of the Soviet Union and the waning of communist ideology, still another form of utopian thinking has asserted itself: the coming of a theocratic society purified of the influences of infidels. In Islamist extremism, for example, commitment to the cause of God's new order may involve launching terrorist attacks directed against anyone who stands in its way. Like other forms of utopian thinking, the idea of a theocracy achieved by terror totally disregards the value of the life of actual human beings for the sake of realizing the perfect society of the future.

Any inventory of contemporary utopias would have to include at least one more: the utopia of empire. Empire is the form of utopian thinking that is perhaps the most tempting to the United States today as the world's only superpower, at least for the time being. A growing literature in our time raises the question whether we have entered the age of the American Empire, the *Pax Americana*, with all the dangers that accompany that status. Our coinage bears the motto, "In God we trust," but our temptation to unilateralism in foreign policy and our soaring military budget suggests that our real trust is in large armies and sophisticated weapons. According to the utopia of empire, the United States will secure the future not only for its inhabitants but for all the world, guaranteeing safety, prosperity, and peace for generations to come by extending its ideals, its way of life, and its economic and military domination to all parts of the globe.

All of these images of hope, whether the conflicting utopias of individualism and collectivism or the embattled utopias of empire and terrorism, offer no real hope at all. They are all destructive ideologies. Individualism contributes to the dehumanization of life by exalting individual interests at the expense of the common welfare. Collectivist and terrorist ideologies contribute to the dehumanization of life by sacrificing persons in the name of abstract principles and ideals such as the classless society or the theocratic state. Imperial ideology contributes to the dehumanization of life by countering all opposition to its dream of world domination with practices that merely mimic the evils the empire supposedly removes.

Trinitarian faith expresses a genuinely humanizing understanding of God and of the future to which all creation is called. Shunning indifference to the common welfare, which is characteristic of individualism, and rejecting recourse to violence, which is characteristic of terrorism and the counterterrorism of empire, we can hope, pray, and struggle for the future opened by the triune God. The triune God is being-in-communion. Father, Son, and Spirit are united in their mutually self-giving and mutually indwelling love. The life of God is community in which differences are celebrated and love reigns. In the divine society power consists not in domination and control over others but in mutual giving and receiving. So understood, the doctrine of the Trinity bears witness to the coming reign of God inaugurated by Jesus.

Thus the Trinitarian understanding of God defines the power at work in God's coming reign as different. Informed by the doctrine of the Trinity, the Christian view of the fulfillment of human life has profound political, economic, and social implications. It gives unequivocal support to an open and inclusive church and an open and inclusive society. It gives encouragement to democratic as opposed to totalitarian government. It would be foolish, of course, to suggest that the doctrine of the Trinity provides a blueprint for all societies and governments to follow. Nevertheless, it is a vision of God's coming reign that disrupts our present way of life and that can inspire creative social efforts that honor the dignity and rights of all, that favor the common good over cutthroat competition, and that work toward a more just distribution of opportunity and wealth.

If the power of the triune God is the power of community-forming love, and if the triune God enters freely into the suffering of creation for the sake of its renewal and completion, then not only the world but the very life of God has a history and a goal. As noted earlier in chapter 3, the Old Testament prophets announce the coming of a new exodus (Isa. 43:18–19). God will create a new heaven and a new earth (65:17). God's justice and peace shall reign throughout the earth (11:1–9). Hope permeates the New Testament as well. While the New Testament witnesses confess the fulfillment of God's promises in

Jesus Christ, they also eagerly look ahead to the completion of God's purposes throughout the creation. According to the book of Revelation, the one who sits upon the throne promises, "See, I am making all things new" (Rev. 21:5). Not even God already enjoys the new heaven and the new earth. God is not yet "everything to every one" (1 Cor. 15:28 RSV). So great is the divine love that the shining of the glory of God in all the world will be complete only when the creation is set free from all sin and suffering, and set free for everlasting life in the communion, peace, and joy of the triune God.

## Questions for Discussion

1. In what ways does the interpretation of the doctrine of the Trinity in this chapter help you to understand what this doctrine is all about and why it is important for the witness and life of the church?
2. Why is the presence of suffering and evil in the world so troubling to Christians? If we can't resolve the mystery of suffering and evil, what can we do?
3. How do you understand the statement that "not even God already enjoys the new heaven and the new earth"? In what sense does God's work of creation and redemption add to the glory of God?

# The Reshaping of Power in Christian Life

*Faith, hope, and love abide . . . and the greatest of these is love*
(1 Cor. 13:13)

## Faith in God and the Power to Forgive

Does it make any difference what understanding we have of God's power? Does our understanding of God affect the way we see the world and the way we view ourselves? Is it really important for our everyday life and practice whether the ultimate power in whom we trust is arbitrary and coercive—the spirit of God-almightiness—or the power of the triune God who creates, saves, and renews? I have insisted all along that it does make a difference, an immeasurable difference. The difference is practical as well as theoretical. It shows itself in the way we think and act not only on Sundays but also on the other days of the week, not only in our worship and prayer but also in our business transactions and political decisions.

In this chapter, I want to be more specific about the difference faith in the triune God makes in the everyday life of Christians. As I have noted on more than one occasion, it makes little sense to think of the life of the individual Christian or the corporate life of the church as a "power-free zone."[1] A different kind of power, a different exercise of power, yes; the sheer absence or rejection of power, no. What can we say, then, about the different power at work in Christian life? How is human power reshaped by the power of God?

Christian life is described by Paul as a life of faith, hope, and love (1 Cor. 13:13). In the theological tradition these are called the three theological "virtues." They are added to the four cardinal "virtues" of classical Greek ethics: wisdom, justice, temperance, and courage. While philosophical ethics describes virtues as human dispositions toward the good, in Christian theology the theological virtues are not inherent human abilities or powers. They are powers of a new humanity made possible by the grace of God alone. By the free gift of Christ and the working of his Spirit, human life comes to full stature in faith, hope, and love.

As *gifts of God*, faith, hope, and love are nevertheless also our free *human* acts. They are both *God's* doing and *our* doing. How can that be? The answer is that God's action and human action are not mutually exclusive. On the contrary, we are most truly human when we are dependent on the grace of God. The grace of God brings us to our true humanity. It does not run over us like a bulldozer, or turn us into lifeless puppets dangling from strings moved by an unseen puppeteer. Awakened to new life by the grace of God in Jesus Christ and the working of the Holy Spirit, we are both empowered and called to new freedom and responsibility as servants, children, and friends of God.

Let us begin with the virtue of faith and ask once more what it means to have faith in God. Faith is letting God be God. It is placing our whole trust in God, who is decisively made known in Jesus Christ and at work in the world by his Spirit. Faith is relying on God alone not as sheer power but as the loving power who has created us, who forgives our sins, and who renews us for a life of service of God and our neighbor.

Trust in God brings both relief from an immense burden and a new power to live as God intends us to live. When we live by faith, we are relieved of the terrible burden of "playing God." The God we try to imitate when we "play God" is not God at all but the product of our own pride, fear, and self-deception. When we trust in the living God, we are freed from the desire and need to be omnipotent. We are liberated from the fear that we must amass as much power as possible so that we can control others who are out to control us. We are freed from the self-deception that clings to our sense of innocence and righteousness and refuses to admit our need of forgiveness.

Faith as trust in the gracious power of God in Jesus Christ not only brings *freedom from* the pretense of being God but also *freedom for* the service of God and others. Faith is not only the thankful acceptance of God's forgiveness but also the beginning of a life of forgiving others. In a broken and sinful world, the power of forgiveness, rooted in faith in God who freely forgives, is the power of new beginnings.[2]

The logic of Christian faith is simple. Just as God has forgiven us, we are to forgive one another (Eph. 4:32). Just as God's forgiveness is free and extravagant, ours should be free and generous also. "How often should I forgive? As many as seven times?" Peter asks Jesus. And Jesus replies, "Not seven times, but . . . seventy-seven times" (Matt. 18:21–22). When the gift of forgiveness is actually lived out, the results are stunning. In October 2006 the Amish community of Nickel Mines, Pennsylvania, confounded many Americans and the mass media by forgiving the gunman who invaded a schoolhouse in their town and shot to death five young Amish girls. As the entire community dealt with their grief, the gunman's wife was graciously welcomed at the girls' funeral service. Said one Amish woman, "If you have Jesus in your heart and he has forgiven you . . . how can you not forgive other people?" It sounds simple, but would it have been simple for us if one of our children had been a victim in that schoolhouse?

The church practices the sacrament of baptism as a witness to the forgiving power of God in Jesus Christ and as the beginning of a new life by faith in him. In the Nicene Creed the church declares, "We acknowledge one baptism for the forgiveness of sins." This statement affirms that we are baptized into the life, death, and resurrection of Jesus Christ, who embodies God's gift of forgiveness. It also affirms that the life of all who are baptized into Christ is to be marked by the forgiveness of others. Jesus teaches his disciples to pray, "Forgive us our sins, for we ourselves forgive everyone indebted to us" (Luke 11:4). Trust in God's forgiveness of us and our practice of forgiveness of others go hand in hand. They are related as tree and fruit, as fountain and stream.

The practice of forgiveness is a "virtue," an act of extraordinary power activated by the Spirit of God. When we live by faith, we are both called and empowered to forgive, to engage in the practice of forgiving others because we have been forgiven by God. But is the practice of forgiveness aptly described as an act of power? Isn't it more like being powerless? Not at all. While the act of forgiveness is different from power as control of others, it is far from a display of powerlessness. Rather, it is a participation in and reflection of the creative and redemptive power of God, who freely humbled himself for the salvation of the world. We cannot forgive exactly like God, but in our acts of forgiveness we can take part in and bear witness to God's power of forgiveness and reconciliation and the new life in friendship with others that it makes possible.[3]

When human beings forgive, who is helped? The persons forgiven, or the persons who forgive? The answer is, both. Forgiving is both a giving and a giving up. First and foremost, the act of forgiveness is a gift to those who have committed a wrong. Those forgiven receive a gift, are relieved of a debt, are released from a bondage. But when we forgive someone, we not only give the person forgiven a gift; we also experience release from our own bondage to a spirit of resentment and bitterness. We give up our desire to retaliate against those who have harmed us. We give up the urge to return evil for evil. We conquer the impulse to be vengeful. Although we have been wronged, we do not demand redress. We cancel the debt that is owed us. In the act of forgiveness we relinquish our claims on another. We give up our power to lock others in their prisons of indebtedness and guilt. The truth is that without forgiveness, there is no new life either for the one who has wronged another or for the one who has been wronged.

As a free act of faith, forgiveness is, of course, both risky and costly. It is risky because, in its most radical form, forgiveness is unconditional. On the cross, Jesus prayed, "Father, forgive them; for they do not know what they are doing" (Luke 23:34). How different Jesus' prayer would have been if it had taken the form, "Forgive them if," or "Forgive them on the condition that." Forgiveness is risky because there is no guarantee that our gesture of acceptance will find a healing response from the person whom we have forgiven.

Forgiveness is costly as well as risky. It is costly because in this act we die a little. We give up that part of ourselves that wants to retaliate. In our acts of forgiveness, as in our baptism, we die with Christ in his costly death for us all even as we also participate in his new, risen life.

All human relationships deteriorate and eventually collapse without forgiveness. The importance of forgiveness is evident in family relationships. Family life becomes a tedious or brutal power struggle if the members fail to practice mutual forgiveness. One of every two marriages in the United States ends in divorce. Even when divorce does not occur, statistics indicate that family life is often an ugly battleground. Battered wives and beaten children are evidence of the cruel and destructive exercise of power in the family sphere. In view of the many pressures that bear down on the family in modern society, the future viability of family life depends on the discovery and exercise of a different kind of power in family relationships: the power to forgive that comes from the gracious, forgiving power of God.

God's gift of forgiveness in Jesus Christ exposes abuse of others, whether in family life or in other relationships, as a yearning for omnipotence. Trust in God made known in Jesus Christ and awakened by his Spirit liberates us from this destructive fantasy. It also liberates those who have been abused from the lifelong burden of resentment that can poison one's soul. No doubt there are relationships from which we simply have to detach ourselves. However, whether we stay in or feel compelled to move out of a deeply troubled relationship, forgiveness is essential. If the God in whom we trust is the triune God, we will understand that true human power is the power of life-in-community, and human community is not possible apart from forgiveness. The triune God is not an autonomous self writ large but a God whose life is in communion and who empowers us for relationships in which we are called to forgive others as God has forgiven us.

The practice of this different power called forgiveness that is rooted in faith in God turns out to be as important in the realm of public policy and international relations as in the sphere of personal relationships. During the early years of the postapartheid government in South Africa, the attention of the world was riveted on the work of the Truth and Reconciliation Commission in the new government. It has been called by some the grand political experiment of our time. Instead of promoting retaliation against those who had committed horrible crimes under the apartheid system, President Mandela and religious leaders like Archbishop Desmond Tutu proposed another way: the way of truth telling and forgiveness.

For the commission, forgiveness was not pretending that terrible things did not happen. It was not turning a blind eye to evil. Forgiveness faces reality rather than trying to hide it or deny it. There is no cheap grace, and there is no painless forgiveness. The truth must be told. One woman, whose father had been brutally murdered by police, quietly concluded her testimony to the commission by saying: "We do want to forgive, but we don't know whom to forgive."[4] Amnesty was offered to those offenders who were willing to tell the truth and own up to their crimes. Even if the process of the Truth and Reconciliation Commission was flawed—as many critics have charged—it reminded the new South African nation, and the world at large, of the political indispensability of both truth and forgiveness if there is to be any possibility of new life for a divided nation or a divided world.

To speak of the place of forgiveness in public policy and international relations is not to deny the importance of the demand for justice. Nor is it to deny the necessity and legitimacy of some system of national defense in a world where nations are armed to the teeth. It is, however, to be reminded that neither individuals nor nations can ever flourish apart from the practice of forgiveness. Military supremacy and the capacity for preemptive strikes against nations considered enemies cannot guarantee a safe and peaceful world.

The practice of forgiveness, whether in personal or international relationships, involves risky giving and risky self-limitation for the sake of a new beginning. The world is especially in need of new beginnings in the relationships of Western nations and nations of the Middle East. It is in need of new beginnings in the relationships between affluent nations of the Northern Hemisphere and nations of the Southern Hemisphere that are desperately poor. There can be no new beginnings without acts of generosity, truth telling, and forgiveness for the injuries of the past.

The practice of self-limitation and forgiveness among the nations is of immense importance in a world where the spread of weapons of mass destruction threatens unimaginable devastation and possibly the end of human life on our planet. Unbounded allegiance to the gods of nation, race, and ethnicity severely aggravates the mortal danger these weapons pose. Many people in the West are terrified by the building of an "Islamic" nuclear bomb. Does such language imply that the world would be safe if the weapons of mass destruction were restricted to the "Christian" nuclear bombs in Europe and America, the "Judaic" nuclear bombs in Israel, and the "Hindu" nuclear bombs in India?

Those who trust in the God revealed in the crucified Jesus must surely recoil from the madness of manufacturing and stockpiling weapons of mass destruction. If the God in whom we trust is a God whose creative and redemptive activity consistently displays an altogether different kind of power, we will bear witness to a different way of engaging in international relationships. While recognition of the capacity for mutual destruction may act for a time as a precarious deterrent to nuclear, chemical, or biological warfare, only the willingness to give up imperial ambitions and to practice a different kind of diplomacy, free of malice and ready to forgive and start anew, is strong enough to break the deadly circle of violence and counterviolence.

Being willing to limit our power is also crucial in our relationship to the natural environment and in our use of energy. We have waged war on nature for many generations. For the sake of humanity and especially the poor countries of the world who will bear the brunt of damage to the environment, this war must stop. If we trust in God, we will care for the natural order as God cares for it. God calls us to stewardship in our use of natural resources. This requires responsible exercise of power. Evidence of the earth's warming as a result of unchecked burning of carbon fuels is now irrefutable. Air, land, and water are heavily polluted in many parts of the globe. To continue to assault nature in this wanton way is a betrayal of the wisdom of the gospel. Any defense of the reckless treatment of nature under the pretense that humanity has been given dominion over the earth by God has nothing to do with Christian faith. It is superficial piety used in the interests of the privileged few. God acts noncoercively in creating the heavens and the earth and in freely becoming a humble servant for our salvation. Faith in this God will be manifest in our time in the strength of creative restraint. Both in international relations and in our use of natural resources, our readiness for self-limitation and our practice of forgiveness are of crucial importance both for the present generation and for the life of generations to come.

## Love of God and the Power to Welcome Strangers

Of the three great "virtues" of Christian life, Paul says that love is the greatest (1 Cor. 13:13). Asked which was the greatest commandment, Jesus gave the twofold answer: First, "You shall love the Lord your God with all your heart, and with all your soul, and with all your mind, and with all your strength"; and second, "You shall love your neighbor as yourself" (Mark 12:30–31).

We should not take this twofold love commandment of Jesus out of its larger context in the gospel narrative. If the story of Jesus is rightly understood, it says clearly that love is first of all the gift of God in Jesus and only then a command that Jesus gives to us. Like all the "virtues" or powers of Christian life, love is first of all a gift we receive from God. We love because God first loved us. "God so loved the world that he gave his only Son" (John 3:16). "As I have loved you, you also should love one another" (John 13:34)." "Beloved, since God loved us so much, we also ought to love one another" (1 John 4:11). "God's love has been poured into our hearts through the Holy Spirit that has been given to us" (Rom. 5:5). The order of God's love and our love is absolutely clear. Because "God is love" (1 John 4:8) and because he first loved us, we are called to love. The Christian virtue of love is born and grows as a response to the love of God that is always a step ahead of us.

Our culture has a very sentimental notion of love. The assumption is that everyone is born with a loving disposition that gets messed up by the institutions of society. All the problems of the world would be easily solved, it is presumed, if people would only be true to their own nature and act lovingly toward others. According to a popular song, "All you need is love." The Christian understanding of love is very different. The power to love comes from beyond ourselves, and the practice of love, like the practice of every Christian virtue, requires a lifetime of training. The conversion and transformation of human beings from self-preoccupation to concern for others does not happen in an instant. Christian life is a journey from an old to a new way of life. God gives us time and patiently guides us on this journey, encouraging but also judging us on the way. God's judgment is always purposive and aims to release us from our bondage of self-centeredness to a life centered in love of God and our neighbor.

But how do we love God? By obeying his will, both Old and New Testaments reply. According to Paul, the whole of the law of God is summed up in a single commandment, "You shall love your neighbor as yourself" (Gal. 5:14). Paul is not here contradicting the twofold love commandment of Jesus. He is simply saying that our love of God takes concrete form in our love of neighbor.

The next obvious questions are, Who is our neighbor? and, What form does love of the neighbor take? Jesus answers these questions in his unforgettable parable of the Good Samaritan (Luke 10:25–37). The parable describes the surprising and extravagant care given by a Samaritan to a stranger who had been beaten by robbers and left wounded on the road. A priest and a Levite hurry past the wounded man. When the Samaritan comes along, however, he not only stops to tend the injured man's wounds; he puts him on his own donkey and takes him to an inn. There he pays the innkeeper to care for the man and even promises to return later to pay for whatever additional expenses may be incurred. Jews and Samaritans were estranged people at the time of Jesus, and his parable highlights the fact that the Samaritan's act of love was an act of hospitality to a stranger, even one considered an enemy.

Now we may well ask: Who in the world acts with such extravagant love for a stranger? In the history of the interpretation of this parable, some interpreters have seen in the figure of the Samaritan the person of Jesus himself. He has found humanity wounded and in mortal danger. He has tended our wounds at his own expense and has promised to take responsibility even for our future well-being. We were strangers to him and he to us, but he has treated us with extravagant love and hospitality. This interpretation of the parable should not be quickly dismissed as fanciful. It makes the important point that while we are indeed called by Jesus to be "good Samaritans" and to extend welcome and care to our neighbors—many of whom are strangers—we do this because God in Jesus himself has welcomed and cared for us. "Welcome one another," Paul writes, "just as Christ has welcomed you" (Rom. 15:7). Only from *the* "Good Samaritan" do we receive power to act in correspondence to his hospitality to us.[5]

The theme of hospitality to strangers as a concrete form of the love that God calls us to show to others runs through the entire Bible. Abraham shows hospitality to three strangers, not knowing that it was the Lord who appeared to him in them (Gen. 18). The Israelites are commanded to be hospitable to strangers in the land because they too were once strangers in the land of Egypt (Lev. 19:34). Jesus not only tells parables about hospitality but extends hospitality to strangers in his ministry, dining often with outcasts and people of ill repute. In Jesus' depiction of the day of judgment, he teaches that it will not be those who have simply called him "Lord" every day who will be accounted faithful. Instead, the faithful will be recognized by their service to the needy: "I was hungry and you gave me food, I was thirsty and you gave me something to drink, I was a stranger and you welcomed me, I was naked and you gave me clothing, I was sick and you took care of me, I was in prison and you visited me. . . . Truly I tell you, just as you did it to one of the least of these who are members of my family, you did it to me" (Matt. 25:35–36, 40).

Adding all this together, we have to conclude that Jesus not only calls us to show hospitality to the stranger. He is the stranger who shows hospitality to us, and he is the stranger to whom we show hospitality when we give food to the hungry, water to the thirsty, and shelter to the homeless.

A memorable instance of hospitality to strangers occurred in the little mountain village of Le Chambon in France during the Nazi occupation. Jews were being rounded up all over Europe and sent to concentration camps, where millions of them were killed. In the winter of 1941, a Jewish woman, fleeing from the Nazis, knocked on the door of the home of Pastor Trocmé and his wife and asked for help. The Jewish woman was invited in. In the ensuing months and years, several thousand Jews were hidden by the people of Le Chambon and thereby saved from sure destruction.[6]

Just as faith in God finds an appropriate practice in the act of forgiveness, so love finds a concrete practice in the act of hospitality to strangers. The church is called to lead the way in cultivating this practice. It is called to provide the training ground of a new humanity marked by the virtue of hospitality. Cultivation of the Christian practice of hospitality begins at the Lord's Table and is strengthened by our repeated presence at the table. Celebration of this sacrament is communal practice in the hospitality of God. At this table, where the reconciling work of Christ is recalled, the living Lord is the host extending his hospitality to all. Strangers from every corner of the earth are invited to take part in the life-giving hospitality of the crucified and risen Jesus Christ in the power of his Spirit, and then to share this hospitality with other guests at the table and with strangers beyond.

We live today in a period of unprecedented migration of peoples. More than ever, there are strangers in every land. They come seeking work and the chance to improve their lives and the lives of their families. This worldwide migration is putting an enormous strain on many governments as they contend with the economic challenges and the "culture wars" that inevitably attend the presence of increasing numbers of strangers in their lands. The Christian church is also challenged by this situation. What is the mission of the church in a world of immigrants and strangers?

The call to show hospitality to strangers clashes with the fear and narcissism that holds many people captive today. According to Greek legend, Narcissus fell in love with himself when he saw his reflection in a pool of water. Captivated by his own image, he refused to move for fear of losing his beloved. The myth of Narcissus describes one form of the human condition called sin. As sinners, we are inclined to that excessive self-love that causes us to disregard or fear those unlike us. We become preoccupied with ourselves or with those very much like ourselves. We become paralyzed by fear of strangers.

But isn't there good reason to be fearful of strangers? Wouldn't we be irresponsible if we did not teach our children not to go anywhere with a stranger and not to get in a car with a stranger who offers them a ride? Wouldn't we be irresponsible if we failed to recognize that in our dangerous world nations must have responsible immigration policies? Should we welcome even those who intend to do us harm? Are there no boundaries in calling Christians to welcome strangers?

These are difficult and disturbing questions. Yes, instruction to our children who are not yet able to make good judgments is necessary. We have a responsibility as parents to protect our children from those who would injure them. Yes, a nation has an obligation to protect its citizens from those who intend to do it harm. But in describing Christian love in the concrete language of practicing the welcoming of strangers, our concern is to define the distinctive mission of the church in relation to those who are looked upon as different. What witness should the church bear to the wider society in the matter of hospitality to strangers?

If much in our culture caters to fear of the stranger, suspicion of the stranger all too often finds rich soil in many of our churches as well. But fear and exclusion of strangers contradicts the very nature of the church. The community established and sustained by the love of God in Jesus Christ is joyfully diverse. It does not glory in deadening uniformity. It is called to be an inclusive community and to show hospitality to strangers. When true to its mission, the church hears the instruction of the book of Hebrews: "Do not neglect to show hospitality to strangers, for by doing that some have entertained angels without knowing it" (Heb. 13:2). True Christian community reflects and celebrates the diversity of life that God has created and redeemed. God's own welcoming love empowers the church to show hospitality to those who are different.

A character in Jean-Paul Sartre's play *No Exit* says: "Hell is other people."[7] Nothing could be farther from the Christian gospel than this remark. In the light of Jesus Christ, to be fully human is to be in relationship with God and others. Christian identity is found in a community that is open to and inclusive of the stranger. Growth in Christian life is measured by an increasing ability to affirm the worth of others who are different in important ways from us. To love freely, as God freely loves, is to enter into solidarity with other people, and especially with other people who are considered strangers. The transforming power of God is at work in our lives when we begin to transcend self-interest and reach out in love and friendship to others, especially to those who seem disturbingly different. To reach out in this way is to be enlivened by the "spirit of power and of love" (2 Tim. 1:7), to share in "the power of [Christ's] resurrection" (Phil. 3:10).

The gifts of the Spirit of Christ are not intended to form a closed group bound together by a sense of superiority and self-congratulation. They should increase our sensitivity to others, especially to those who are different from us and perhaps initially suspected as threats to us—the stranger, the immigrant, the handicapped, the poor, the politically or culturally oppressed, all those pushed to the margins of society for whatever reasons. Authentic Christian growth manifests itself in the readiness to help in the building up of new, inclusive human community.

Homogeneity in the Christian community is therefore a contradiction of the gospel of God's omnipotent love, which frees us to accept as brothers and sisters those considered strangers and enemies. A community that calls itself Christian and is complacent about its economic, racial, and cultural insularity is a community without the power of the Spirit.

Some church leaders advocate an outreach program for congregations that would focus on people most similar to their present members. But evangelism that deliberately aims at homogeneity for the sake of church growth is a display of spiritual weakness rather than real spiritual strength. The greatest of the gifts of the Spirit, according to the apostle Paul, is not some sensational power but the power of *agape*, the love that seeks out the different and the unwanted, the love that forgives and receives enemies as friends. Black and white, women and men, young and old, healthy and sick, are made one people by the love of Christ. As Paul writes: "There is no longer Jew or Greek, there is no longer slave or free, there is no longer male and female; for all of you are one in Christ Jesus" (Gal. 3:28). Participation in Christian community should give us a chance to learn the day-to-day meaning of free and glad affirmation of people who are different from us. A policy of apartness, official or unofficial, wherever it is proposed, stands in contradiction to the open, other-affirming love of the triune God.

By saying as I did earlier that the church is called to lead the way in cultivating the practice of hospitality and the other virtues of Christian life, I do not want to indulge in or promote an unrealistic view of the church. The church is far from perfect. To the church's shame, hospitality to the stranger is sometimes more evident outside than inside the church.

Yet with all of its flaws and in all of its finitude, the church is called to be a community in which a new humanity and a new form of human power are being shaped by the grace of God. The church is called to be the sign and vanguard of the coming reign of God. Our human power is judged and transformed as we gather as Christians to hear God's Word, celebrate the sacraments of baptism and the Lord's Supper, provide support and encouragement to one another, and pray for help and guidance as we engage in the service of our neighbors. In worship we are drawn beyond ourselves. Our lives are redirected and our daily practices are transformed. We hear again the gospel story of the crucified and risen Lord, we praise the triune God in hymn and prayer, and we express our trust in and love for the God whose astonishing grace extends to all people.

Nourished and strengthened in Christian community, we are called to reach out in friendship and solidarity with all people, and always especially with people who are neglected and pushed to the margins. The church does not exist for its own sake. It is not a closed circle for a select few. The church is called to be for others, to reach out to others, not out of a spirit of pity and condescension, but out of the strong passion of the triune God for a world of justice, freedom, and peace. Christian life is thus a practice of solidarity with the poor, the exploited, the victims of injustice. The test of the faithfulness of the Christian community is more than a test of right belief (orthodoxy). It is also a test of right practice (orthopraxis). A sure sign of the right practice of love is hospitality to strangers. If the power of God is liberating love, if it frees us to affirm others, Christians will want to express their solidarity with the stranger, the poor, and the abused.

Let there be no mistake. The first victims of every new upward spiral in the military arms race are the poor of the earth. The first casualties of every relaxation of commitment to human rights are the defenseless and the despised people in any society. The first human sacrifices of economic policies designed to make life easier for the rich are the weak and little ones of the world, those whom Christ called his brothers and sisters. The first discards of xenophobic attitudes and punitive immigration policies are the strangers in our midst. Christian love finds expression in many ways. But high on the list of these ways will always be the practice of hospitality to strangers.

### Hope in God and the Power to Pray
### and Labor for God's Coming Reign

The different power of God is the source not only of Christian faith and Christian love but also of Christian hope. Faith is confidence in

God that frees us from efforts to justify ourselves and from the will to gain control over others in order to secure our own life. The gift of faith liberates us for the practice of forgiveness. Love is the gift of God whose own welcome and hospitality enable us to rejoice in communion with others and to practice hospitality to strangers. Hope too is a gift of God, a "virtue" or power of the new life in Christ. It is the eager expectation of the transformation of all things by God. As a gift, hope, like faith and love, is not an inherent possession or capacity of our own. It is not something we possess, like the color of our eyes. Hope is a gift to be freely received and freely practiced and lived out in the everyday.

Living in hope is difficult. That is where we must begin. It is much easier to live in superficial optimism or quiet despair. When our prospects look bleak or when the course of world events seems dire, it is easy enough to say, "Things will get better. They always do. There is always a silver lining to every cloud." Superficial optimism is one alternative to genuine hope. Then there is the opposite alternative. When a fatal disease strikes us or a loved one, our understandable reaction may be anger and resentment, and then perhaps silent resignation to our fate. When our efforts to assist the downtrodden in their struggle for justice meet with repeated failures, it is only natural, and certainly easy, to give up or to turn bitter and cruel. Quiet despair, like cheap optimism, poisons hope.

Christian hope responds differently. It resists every repression or distortion of our yearnings for healing and wholeness in our personal life, and for justice and freedom in our social order. Christian hope fuels the passion for new life and for human flourishing. It strengthens the longing for a new, transformed humanity in a redeemed world. Yet true hope engenders these activities without bravado and without reliance on force.

Christians dare to hope in the power of the crucified and risen Lord whose grace is stronger than all the powers of destruction and death in our world. Because the crucified Lord is risen and his transforming Spirit is at work in the world today, Christians boldly hope—"hoping against hope" (Rom. 4:18)—for the coming triumph of God over all evil. With Paul, they even mock death:

"Death has been swallowed up in victory."
"Where, O death, is your victory?
Where, O death, is your sting?"
(1 Cor. 15:54–55)

This is the voice of hope in God that refuses to become resigned to the way things are, to say in despair: "What's the use? Things will never change." Resurrection hope holds to the promises of God that find their "Yes" in Jesus Christ (2 Cor. 1:20). This hope enlists us in the struggle against all that demeans and destroys life. It encourages us to plead with God—even allows us to protest to God—to hasten the coming of justice and peace, to change what seems unchangeable, to redeem what seems a total loss. Christian hope keeps us restless for God's new world. It allows no more than a provisional consent to suffering, loss, and death. The provisional consent of hope to depths of suffering for which there is at present no healing is very different from resignation. In this provisional consent of hope there is a refusal to give up and simply accept the lordship of injustice and death. Christian hope never consents to suffering and loss for more than the time being, for it dares to trust in a power that changes everything.

That power is the sovereign love of God in Christ Jesus, whose transforming Spirit continues to work in human life and throughout the creation. The strong love of God is the unshakable foundation of Christian hope.

Who will separate us from the love of Christ? Will hardship, or distress, or persecution, or famine, or nakedness, or peril, or sword? . . . No, in all these things we are more than conquerors through him who loved us. For I am convinced that neither death, nor life, nor angels, nor rulers, nor things present, nor things to come, nor powers, nor height, nor depth, nor anything else in all creation, will be able to separate us from the love of God in Christ Jesus our Lord. (Rom. 8:35, 37–39)

The practice of Christian hope is the practice of prayer and work for God's coming kingdom. *Ora et labora*—pray and work—is the motto of many monastic communities, but it is also an appropriate motto for the life of every Christian. Hope and prayer are intertwined. That is clear from the content of the Lord's Prayer, which is primarily a string of petitions. In this prayer we ask that God will let his name be hallowed, let his kingdom come, let his will be done on earth as in heaven. We do not claim to be able to do these things ourselves. We place our hope not in ourselves but in God. In the Lord's Prayer we also pray for our daily bread, for forgiveness, for defense against temptation and all evil forces. Again, we do not claim to be able by ourselves to accomplish these things. We hope in God and place our present and future in God's hands. Out of familiarity, we often forget that the Lord's Prayer is a prayer of radical hope in God.

The practice of Christian prayer, however, cannot be separated from service and work for God's reign. Praying is always to be accompanied by working. Christians do not pray rather than work, or work rather than pray. The practice of Christian hope requires both. Prayer inspires service, and service always begins and ends in prayer.

What does it mean to work for the coming of God's reign? To build the kingdom of God? To usher in the new heaven and new earth? To mount the heavens and bring to earth the new Jerusalem? These ways of speaking of our Christian service say far too much. They contravene recognition of our radical dependence on God that is expressed in the Lord's Prayer. To work and serve in hope is simply to prepare the way for God's coming reign. It is to take small, first steps in the direction of God's new world. It is to bear witness to God's coming reign by creating signs and parables of this reign here and now.

When the Truth and Reconciliation Commission in South Africa opened a new chapter in race relations in that country by taking seriously the need for both truthfulness and forgiveness, what happened was by no means the arrival of God's kingdom. It was, however, a sign and a first step in the direction of a new possibility of human flourishing in South Africa and perhaps elsewhere as well. When Christians from many different denominations traveled to New Orleans to help build homes and civic buildings devastated by hurricane Katrina, these activities did not bring in God's new heaven and new earth. They offered, however, a concrete sign of and a small preparation for God's coming new world marked by justice, peace, and mutual care. When in time of war and threat of war, Christians call on their government to pursue peace diligently and unrelentingly through diplomacy, "even at risk to national security" (as the Presbyterian Confession of 1967 says), and when Christians work to increase understanding among peoples of different nations, cultures, and religions, such acts of witness do not usher in God's kingdom. They may constitute, however, a preparation for God's new world. They may offer parables of its coming to a world so much in need of hope. It is one of the tasks of the church to use what opportunities are available at any given time to sow seeds of hope by creating signs and parables of God's coming reign.

Christian hope in God who raised the crucified Jesus from the dead has some distinguishing marks. One is its inclusiveness. This means, first of all, that Christian hope embraces both the living and the dead. The Christian vision of the future does not regard the dead as mere stepping-stones to a future paradise built solely by human effort. Christian hope does not concede the final victory to death. As God raised the crucified Jesus from the dead, so God's promise of new life is far greater than we can imagine. Our hope is based finally not on ourselves, or on what we can accomplish with our deeds of love, or on our social and political programs of reform and renewal, but on the gracious God who brings into existence things that did not exist and who raises the dead to fellowship in the coming kingdom (Rom. 4:17).

A second aspect of the inclusiveness of Christian hope is that it embraces both humanity and the whole of creation. Christian hope is a breathtakingly inclusive hope rather than a small or partial hope. Neither individuals in themselves nor even humanity as a whole exhausts God's plan of salvation. As we hope in solidarity with all of our suffering and dying brothers and sisters, we also hope in solidarity with the entire cosmos made by God and destined for transformation. Such hope makes an important difference in our everyday decisions and practices. If we dare to hope not only for the living but also for the dead and for future generations, if we dare to hope not only for people like ourselves but for all people, if we dare to hope not only for the human race but for the whole of creation as well—we will repent of all petty visions of the future. We will refuse to draw closed circles around ourselves and people like us. With Paul, Christians will express solidarity in hope with the whole groaning creation that restlessly awaits God's coming redemption (Rom. 8:21–23).

Possibly the most eloquent expression of daring human hope in the past century is the speech of Martin Luther King Jr., delivered in Washington, D.C., in August 1963 and entitled "I Have a Dream."[8] King had a global vision of justice and peace. He dreamed of an end to racial discrimination and the exploitation of the poor. In his dream he saw a time when free men and women, of all colors, cultures, and national origins, would live in harmony with one another. The dream that King shared with millions of people and for which he struggled until struck down by an assassin's bullet was profound and moving. The "God of hope" (Rom. 15:13) inspires such dreams.

Another distinguishing aspect of Christian hope is its rejection of escapism. There is a facsimile of hope abroad in church and society today that is narrow and escapist. Escapist hope makes doctrinaire predictions of the end of the world in the near future and describes this end in as terrifying a manner as possible. The narrow appeal of such hope is: Believe in Jesus and you will be one of the fortunate few who will be snatched to safety in the rapture when the horrible events of the final tribulation begin. These predictions that history will soon end in cataclysmic conflagration, together with the assurance that Christians will be spared these horrors, are distortions of authentic Christian hope. Jesus himself denied knowing when the end would come (Mark 13:32). Contemporary prophets of doom apparently know more than Jesus. Martin Luther is said to have declared that if told that Christ was coming tomorrow, he would still plant a tree today. Christians are not called to make predictions about the end time, but to pray "Come, Lord Jesus!" (Rev. 22:20) and to work in the meantime for greater justice and peace as signs of his coming reign.

Still another distinguishing mark of Christian hope is its refusal to endorse violence to reach its goal. If we dare to hope in God revealed in Jesus Christ, we will practice our hope in a nonviolent manner. We will refuse to go the way either of resignation or of violence to achieve what we consider noble goals. Resignation is hopeless, and violence only breeds more violence. While Christian hope keeps alive the struggle for justice, peace, and freedom, it refuses to contribute to the spirit of retaliation and revenge. In faith and hope, Christians are called to bear witness to the "more excellent way" of love (1 Cor. 12:31).

Christian hope is practiced in the search for peace and justice among the nations, peace and justice among the races, peace and justice between women and men, peace and justice between humanity and nature. Peace can be realized only when the spirit of possession is replaced by the spirit of mutual gift giving, when individualism is replaced by the joy of life in community, when differences enrich rather than divide. Peace is not the mere absence of war. It is the dynamic and creative presence of life in friendship with God and others. Peace reigns where the spirit of concern for the well-being of all triumphs over every will to power and will to possession. Christians live and struggle in hope for this peace and justice of the coming reign of God.

A Christian trusts, a Christian loves, a Christian hopes. In and through all of these, a Christian will "pray without ceasing" (1 Thess. 5:17). Prayer is a participation in the different power of God. In prayer we give thanks that the omnipotent love of God, embodied decisively in Jesus Christ and at work in us and in the world here and now by the Holy Spirit, is greater than all the kingdoms and powers of this world. In prayer we ask God for daily bread and for forgiveness—for all that makes human life human. In prayer we refuse to accept injustice as inevitable and commit ourselves to challenge it with all the resources at our disposal. But we also refuse to use coercive means to make the world change according to our timetable. In prayer we learn patience and wait on God. In prayer we receive new strength to continue the struggle for justice and freedom, for a more peaceful world. Thus is human power reshaped by the altogether different power of the triune God—the Father Almighty, the Lord Jesus Christ, and the Holy Spirit, the Giver of Life. To this God we gladly ascribe "the kingdom and the power and the glory, forever."

With this familiar doxology, we have almost reached the end of our exploration of the different power of God. One final step remains: Does our description of the reshaping of human power by the power of the God who freely loves help us to come to terms with the religious pluralism of our world? Can it acknowledge the sad fact that religious commitments are sometimes sources of hatred and violence? Specifically, does it offer any way forward in the new and challenging encounter of Christianity and Islam?

## Questions for Discussion

1. What difference has the power of forgiveness made in your life or in the lives of people you know?
2. In what ways has your own church demonstrated, or in what ways might it demonstrate, the working of the Spirit of God in its midst by welcoming strangers?
3. Do Christians "build the kingdom of God," or do they pray and prepare for the coming of God's reign by taking "small, first steps" in its direction? What is the difference?

7

# Toward a Christian-Muslim Dialogue on the Power of God

*People will bring into [the new Jerusalem] the glory and the honor of the nations*
(Rev. 21:26)

*T*he new encounter between Christianity and Islam is the great religious fact of our time. Coexisting for almost fourteen hundred years, these two faith communities have related to each other in ways that have occasionally been peaceful, sometimes belligerent, and almost always marked by misunderstanding, suspicion, and fear. While the encounter of these two religions has a long history, it has today a new urgency. For one thing, it is taking place worldwide. It is no longer a matter of Christians and Muslims living in separate countries thousands of miles apart. The world has shrunk. Increasingly, Christians and Muslims in the United States and Europe live in the same towns, go to the same schools, and work at the same places.

Beyond demographics, however, events of our own time have catapulted Christianity and Islam into a new, complex, and highly charged encounter. The terrorist attacks on the New York Trade Center and the Pentagon on 9/11; the subsequent wars in Iraq and Afghanistan with all their cruelty and bloodletting; the suicide bombings in London, Madrid, and other cities; the continuing Palestinian-Israeli conflict—these and other events virtually guarantee that Christian-Muslim relationships will be burdened by unrelieved suspicion and most likely deep hostility for many years to come.

Adding to the problem is the lack of preparation that the Christian church and Christian theology bring to this new and complex engagement with Islam. We lack even a working consensus about what the goals of the Christian community and Christian theology should be in this encounter, let alone what are the best means to achieve these goals.

In principle at least, Christians and Muslims should be able to share two goals. The first is ethical: a common commitment to peace and justice among all peoples of the world. The second is theological: a common effort to achieve greater understanding of each other's faith. One of the most important aspects of this theological task is the clarification of what these two great faith traditions have in common and where they diverge in their understandings of God and God's power. In the new encounter between Christianity and Islam, we must get beyond both the perpetuation of stereotypes that stop dialogue and the avoidance of real differences in dialogue. The question I want to explore in this chapter is: What might the Christian church have to learn and what witness might the church have to make about the power of God as Christianity and Islam unavoidably meet once again in our time? I will focus on three topics that are bound to play a part in any theological engagement of Christianity and Islam today: the Word of God and the task of interpretation, the oneness of God and the danger of idolatry, and the triune God and the vision of new community.

## The Word of God and the Task of Interpretation

Like Christianity, Islam has its sacred scriptures. Muslims consider the Qur'an the holiest of books.[1] It contains the revelation of God that is the ultimate authority on all matters of faith and life in Islam. Delivered to Muhammad by the angel Gabriel, the Qur'an is considered the literal word of God. Whatever the Qur'an teaches is definitive and without error. It is the unquestionable truth because its words are the very words of God.

According to the Qur'an, God is absolutely sovereign. He is "powerful and almighty" (58:21).[2] He exercises dominion over all things. Whatever power human beings have derives entirely from him. "God, holder of all control. You give control to whoever you will, and remove it from whoever you will. You elevate whoever you will, and humble whoever you will. All that is good lies in your hand. You have power over everything" (3:26). The Qur'an describes God as radically transcendent but also as closer to humans than their "jugular vein" (50:16).

Some Christians assume that the Qur'an's understanding of God's omnipotence is completely deterministic and makes no room for human freedom and responsibility. This assumption is false. If the Qur'an emphasizes God's sovereignty and human dependence, parallels to such affirmations can easily be found in both the Old and New Testaments. The relationship of divine governance and human freedom has long been a subject of debate in Islamic theology as it has in Christian theology. According to the distinguished Muslim scholar Fazlur Rahman, the Qur'an does not view God and humanity as rivals. If one school of Muslim theology (Ash'arite) tends to deny human power to safeguard the omnipotence of God, another school (Mu'tazilite) makes room for human reason and agency. "The Qur'an," Rahman says, "affirms both sides of the tension."[3] According to the Qur'an, "Anything good that happens to you is from God; anything bad is from yourself" (4:79). This statement bears some resemblance to the apostle Paul's "not I, but the grace of God that is with me" (1 Cor. 15:10), which the Christian theologian Donald Baillie famously described as the "paradox of grace."[4]

A particularly noteworthy example of the Qur'anic effort to make room for human freedom and thus to balance divine omnipotence and human responsibility is the story of God's command to Abraham to sacrifice his beloved son, Isaac. In the Hebrew text of Genesis 22, not a word is said about what Isaac thinks and wills when he discovers he is the one to be sacrificed. So glaring is this omission in the biblical text that Martin Luther, commenting on the passage, feels compelled to admonish Moses for leaving out this important detail. In the Qur'an's telling of the story, the consent of the boy (understood by Muslims to be Ishmael rather than Isaac) is decisive. Abraham says: "My son, I have seen myself sacrificing you in a dream. What do you think?" The boy tells his father to obey God's command. "You will find me steadfast," he says.[5]

While speaking of God as having power over all things, the Qur'an does not describe God as a capricious tyrant. On the contrary, it regularly refers to God as merciful and compassionate. With one exception, each of the 114 suras of the Qur'an begins with the invocation: "In the name of Allah, the merciful, the compassionate." Not only in this repeated invocation but in the content of the Qur'an as a whole, God's mercy is a major theme. The title "the merciful one" belongs to God alone. No one is merciful like him.

At the same time, the Qur'an teaches that the God of mercy is also the God of justice. The righteous earn God's rewards and the wicked his wrath. The human life span is a time of testing and is to be lived with utmost moral seriousness. A final day of judgment awaits all when God will exercise exacting justice according to one's good and evil deeds.

If the depiction of God in the Qur'an is complex, equally so is its teaching about the use of force. Like the Christian Scriptures, the Qur'an says many things about power, violence, and war, some of which stand in great tension with each other. One can find in the Qur'an statements like: "When the forbidden months are over, wherever you find the idolaters, kill them, seize them, besiege them, wait for them at every lookout post" (9:5). This passage was quoted by Osama bin Laden in a *fatwa,* or judgment, published in an Arabic newspaper in 1998.[6] Other texts in the Qur'an, however, point in a very different direction. Sura 2:256, sometimes called the most important text offering support of Islamic tolerance of other religions, states: "There is no compulsion in religion."

What about the teaching of jihad in the Qur'an? Many Islamic scholars make at least two important points in response to this question. The first is that it is seriously misleading simply to equate jihad and "holy war." The meaning of jihad is multivalent. It can mean one's "struggle" or "exertion" to conform to the will of God, the arduous effort to discipline oneself and obey the divine commandments. But jihad can also mean the use of force in battle. In one passage of the hadith (reports of Muhammad's deeds and teachings), Muhammad distinguishes between the use of force in battle (called the minor jihad) and the exertion to comply with the commandments of God (called the major jihad).

A second point made by Qur'anic scholars is that many references to use of force in battle in the Qur'an have to do with defensive rather than aggressive war. "Fight in God's cause against those who fight you, but do not overstep the limits. God does not love those who overstep the limits" (2:190). If jihad is understood as defensive war waged within certain limits, it roughly parallels the theory of "just war" in the Christian theological and ethical tradition, according to which war is justly waged only under certain circumstances, for example, when a nation goes to war because it has been attacked (*ius ad bellum*), and when war is waged within particular restrictions, such as the protection of noncombatants (*ius in bello*). If the jihad tradition has been subject to abuse in Islam, the just war tradition has also been misused in Christendom.

The Muslim scholar Abdullahi Ahmed An-na'im draws the following conclusions from his survey of the Qur'an on the use of force by Muslims against non-Muslims. First, in the earlier Meccan period when the new religion was not yet firmly established, we find verses enjoining freedom of choice in religious belief. This contrasts with more aggressive passages from the later Medinan period when Islam had achieved power. Second, there is a progression from use of force in self-defense to use of force in extending Islam. Third, the claim that the Qur'an's understanding of jihad is completely nonviolent cannot be sustained.[7]

The dispute about jihad is only part of the ferment in Islam today. Islam is being pulled in many different directions. Fundamentalists repudiate all Western influence and are prepared to use any means to purify Islam and establish an Islamic theocracy in all its territories. Traditionalists share many of the same goals but reject some of the tactics of the fundamentalists. Reformists call for a discriminating appropriation of some of the principles of Western democracy insofar as they are in essential harmony with Islamic tradition.[8] According to the Reformists, the opening of Islam to democrary and tolerance must draw deeply from its own sacred texts. It will require a fresh retrieval of Qur'anic teaching for new times and circumstances.[9]

What can Christians learn from their encounters with Islam about the use and abuse of sacred scriptures in relation to questions of power and violence? Christians will be compelled to ask anew: How do *we* interpret our sacred texts? Is every text of Scripture taken in isolation the literal words of God? Or must we understand individual texts in their historical and literary contexts and in the light of Scripture's own central message or overarching story of God's dealings with humanity?

All sacred texts, complex and tension-filled as they are, must be interpreted. They require a community of interpretation in which, under the guidance of the Spirit of God, Scriptures are diligently studied and vigorously debated as well as cherished and received as normative for faith and life. The history of exegesis, both in Islam and Christianity, shows that sacred scriptures are not limited to a single interpretation but offer a range of interpretive possibilities. We should not be surprised, therefore, if Muslim interpreters differ in their understanding of Qur'anic texts that speak of the legitimacy of violence against enemies of Islam. Internal debates in the Christian community about what Scripture says on controversial issues are a familiar feature of the history of the church as well. American Christians in the mid-nineteenth century differed widely in their readings of Scripture on the issue of slavery, and Christians worldwide today differ widely in the importance that they assign to scriptural texts that condemn all homosexual behavior as an abomination.

If we cannot avoid the task of interpretation of scriptural texts, the basic question becomes that of the criteria that we employ to arrive at a proper understanding of a particular text. For the Christian community, one essential criterion of scriptural interpretation is that particular texts must be illumined by the central subject matter of Scripture and by Scripture's primary purpose as recognized by the community of faith under the guidance of the Spirit of God. All this is to say that Christians do not, or should not, read Scripture in a vacuum. The church has a history of communal guidance in the interpretation of Scripture. This is one important way dogmas and confessions of faith, and to a lesser extent the whole Christian exegetical tradition, function in the life of the community. Arrived at after much deliberation and debate and with prayer for the guidance of the Spirit of God, they constitute the collective witness of the Christian church to a right reading and understanding of its Scripture.

How should Christians read Scripture? Never in contradiction to the rule of love, says Augustine. Always keeping in mind the doctrine of justification by faith alone, says Luther. Always guided by the Creed, says Roman Catholic theologian Nicholas Lash: "What the Scriptures say at length, the Creed says briefly."[10] Karl Barth warns of "the irremediable danger of consulting Holy Scripture apart from the center," that is, apart from Jesus Christ. If Scripture is read apart from him, Barth contends, "the Scripture principle will not stand very long."[11] If all this be true, then an open Christian theological encounter with Islam today will be ready to hear that Islam too has a long and continuing tradition of Qur'anic exegesis. It too has a communal context of study, debate, and prayer for a responsible understanding and application of its sacred texts as they bear on the question of God's power and the appropriateness or inappropriateness of the use of force in particular circumstances.

The status accorded the Qur'an in Islam raises questions that Christians must address to themselves. How do Christians relate their understanding of the incarnation of God in Jesus Christ to their understanding of biblical authority? The counterpart to the Christian doctrine of the incarnate Word in Islam is not an Islamic doctrine of Muhammad. While he is revered as the foremost and final prophet of God, Muhammad is not considered divine by Islam. If anything compares to the Christian doctrine of incarnation in Islam, it is the Islamic doctrine of the Qur'an. While Scripture is readily acknowledged by Christians as the primary and reliable witness to God's will and purpose culminating in the incarnation of God's Word in Jesus of Nazareth, Scripture cannot itself be equated with the incarnate Word, who is Emmanuel, God with us.

Christians who contend there is an exact equation between what Scripture says and what God says fail to read Scripture in the light of its witness to Christ, and will sooner or later face questions about texts of violence in the Bible similar to those they would raise about some Qur'anic texts. How, for example, does one deal with a text like 1 Samuel 15:2–3, in which Yahweh issues a command to wipe out the enemies of Israel, man, woman, child, and beast? Or how does one interpret a text like Deuteronomy 20:16–17, which calls for the annihilation of everything that breathes in towns located in the territory given to God's chosen people? Is there any doubt that the book of Revelation contains holy war imagery and disturbing cries for vengeance that need to be carefully interpreted? When Christians enter into dialogue with Islam over issues of the power of God and God's attitude toward acts of violence, they will need to ask themselves serious questions about the principles that guide faithful interpretation of their own scriptural texts.

One of the most hopeful developments today in the encounter of the Abrahamic faiths—Judaism, Christianity, and Islam—is the practice by some members of these faith traditions of reading and studying their respective scriptures together in small groups. This is beginning to happen both among groups of laypeople and among scholars.[12] Reading together the story of the call of Abraham, or the binding of Isaac, or the psalms of David may offer fresh insights to all participants into their distinctive uses of Scripture and the distinctive principles of scriptural interpretation that they employ. The Word of God comes to us through human witnesses and requires continuing interpretation. Both Christians and Muslims can learn from and challenge each other as they interpret individual texts and passages not in isolation but in relationship to and in the light of their understanding of the central purpose and message of their sacred texts. Is it not high time for both Christianity and Islam to uncover the sources of violence in their own traditions and to drink deeply from the wells of their own sacred texts that call for faithful witness to God in lives that reject the way of violence in pursuit of justice and peace?

## The Oneness of God and the Danger of Idolatry

In a dramatic break with its past relationships with Islam, the Roman Catholic Church at Vatican II declared that the church "looks with esteem" on the Muslims who "adore one God, living and enduring, merciful and all-powerful, Maker of heaven and earth and Speaker to men."[13]

Islam is passionately monotheistic. Its core teaching is affirmation of the oneness of Allah (*tawid*). As stated in Sura 112: "Say, God is one, God is eternal. He begot no one, nor was he begotten. No one is comparable to him." The profession of God's oneness is the "straight path" of Islam (6:161). The Qur'an teaches that Jews and Christians have also been taught to believe in one God by their Scriptures, the Torah and the Gospel. According to the Qur'an, however, Jews and Christians have misunderstood and corrupted their own Scriptures and, especially in the case of Christians, have deviated from the teaching of the absolute oneness of Allah.

Islam calls Jews and Christians "People of the Book," and summons them to acknowledge along with Muslims the oneness of Allah. "Say, People of the Book, let us arrive at a statement that is common to us all. We worship God alone, we ascribe no partner to him, and none of us takes others beside God as lords. If they turn away, say: 'Witness our devotion to him'" (3:64).

Confession of the oneness of Allah, together with the acknowledgment of Muhammad as Allah's final prophet, is the first and most important of the "five pillars" of Islam (confession, prayer, fasting, alms, and pilgrimage). The only sin that cannot be forgiven is "associating something with God." This is the sin of *shirk* or idolatry. To bear witness to the oneness of God is to reject every idea of a similarity between God and creature as absolutely impossible. Islam thus understands itself as radical and uncompromising monotheism. Allah is uniquely one, and this precludes any notion of multiple deities or of creatures sharing in the being of the one God. According to Islam, God is indeed radically different.

Once we grasp the fundamental significance of the doctrine of the oneness of God as taught by the Qur'an, the basic objections of Islam to Christian teachings are entirely coherent. These objections, already stated in the early disputes between Muslims and Christians, have continued into the modern period. We can summarize them as follows.

First, Islam rejects the doctrine of the Trinity. The confession of three persons in God is tantamount, in Islamic perspective, to tritheism. "Do not speak of a 'Trinity,'" the Qur'an warns (4:171). In the early polemical writing, it seems that Muslim theologians understood the Christian Trinity to consist of God, Mary, and Jesus their son. Later, however, Muslim arguments against Trinitarian doctrine were better informed but equally uncompromising.

Second, Islam rejects the doctrine of the deity of Jesus. This follows logically from the Islamic understanding of the oneness of God. God has no partner. God is not divided and no creature is equal to God or can be associated with God. "He is God the one. God the eternal. He begot no one, and he is not begotten! No one is comparable to him" (112).

Third, Islam rejects the Christian teaching that Jesus Christ the Son of God was crucified for the salvation of the human race. Indeed, the Qur'an denies that Jesus was put to death by crucifixion (4:157). The idea of the execution of Jesus and especially ascribing saving significance to this event clashes with the Islamic understanding of the dignity of a prophet and the omnipotence and transcendence of the one and only God. There is no need for an atoning sacrifice. It is enough for the Lord to forgive the sin of the penitent.

Orthodox Christians, of course, will not agree either with Islam's rejection of the deity of Christ and his saving work or with Islam's repudiation of the Trinitarian understanding of God. Christians will thus have the task of explaining the meaning of these doctrines in a manner consistent with the affirmation of the oneness of God to which they say they hold as tenaciously as do Muslims. I will say more about Trinitarian faith in a moment.

Just now, however, I am interested in underscoring what Christians have to hear in Islam's emphasis on the oneness of God and its accompanying rejection of all idolatry. In effect, Islam calls for rigorous adherence to the first commandment of the Decalogue: "You shall have no other gods before me" (Exod. 20:3). The faith of Islam in the sole lordship of God echoes the central Jewish confession or Shema: "Hear, O Israel: The LORD is our God, the LORD alone" (Deut. 6:4). It also calls to mind the first of the two love commandments of Jesus: "You shall love the Lord your God with all your heart, and with all your soul, and with all your mind, and with all your strength" (Mark 12:30). If Islam is radical monotheism, and if radical monotheism means the sole lordship of God, Christians cannot diverge from this teaching without abandoning their own faith. In the midst of the confessing church's struggle in Nazi Germany, Karl Barth called the first commandment the axiom of all theology that claims to be Christian.

Christians might just be able to hear in Islam's repeated affirmation of the sole lordship of God a call to repentance. This might well take the form of a call for greater care and precision in Christian talk about the Trinity.[14] But the call to repentance that might emerge from an encounter with Islam is not limited to a summons to theological precision. It extends to the way Christians, like people of other faiths or no faith, more often than not fail to practice an uncompromising rejection of *shirk* or idolatry. I give two examples of dangers among some groups of Christians in the United States of, in the words of the Qur'an, "associating something with God."

The first example is the close bond forged between the Christian gospel and a form of American civil religion. A church and theology centered on the gospel of the crucified and risen Christ and its attendant proclamation of a different power of God can only call this religious adornment of American nationalism, idolatry. The church must be ready to ask: Has it been sufficiently critical of interpretations of Christian faith that use it for nationalistic, racial, or class purposes? If not, might the church have something to learn from the warning of Islam not to associate any creature or any power with the one and only Lord? Has "God bless America" become the new liturgy of some American Christians, and is confusion between Christian faith and uncritical allegiance to the state an ever present danger? Should we be concerned if members of a congregation decide that the most appropriate response to the attacks on 9/11 is to install an American flag in the sanctuary?

A second example is the quasi-religious zeal with which some American leaders have taken up the task of extending American-brand democracy to other parts of the world, even justifying the use of force to do so. Might the idea of "democracy," and the conviction that it is imperative to spread the American version of it around the world, function as an idol to which all are obliged to bow down, cost what it may? The words of H. Richard Niebuhr, distinguished American theologian of the last century, are still timely:

> Faith in the Father of Jesus Christ is no more compatible with religious reliance on the good will and power of all the people than with such reliance on a monarchic individual or an aristocratic class. When democracy, instead of being a limited and pragmatic device of government, becomes a religion, when the people begin to worship themselves as though they were their own beginning and their own end, when they are not obedient to a law higher than themselves but regard their wishes or ideals as the source of the moral law, when the people become the measure of all things—then faith must challenge democracy.[15]

I am suggesting that the deep wisdom of the Christian faith that God alone is God and that nothing should be allowed to compete with our unconditional allegiance to God may, paradoxically, be renewed by a serious encounter of Christianity with Islam and its relentless critique of idolatry.

I do not say that Islam has no need to engage in some self-criticism of its own failures to withstand the temptation of idolatry in the form of confusing the power of God with the power of a state or a religious movement. I am simply following the instruction of Jesus to first pluck out the log from one's own eye before wanting to take out the speck in one's neighbor's eye (Matt. 7:3). In its new encounter with Islam, a repentant and humble church may be able to hear needful and helpful words from an unexpected source. Even if Christians may believe that these words from unexpected sources are only fragments of the truth, they are nonetheless important to hear and take to heart. The church should open itself to repentance and reform as it hears an important and needful element of truth in Islam's confession of the sole lordship of God and its uncompromising opposition to all idolatry. God's power is different. It should never be confused or "associated" with any of the vaunted powers of this world, whether nation, race, or way of life.

## The Triune God and the Vision of New Community

In its own unmistakable way, Islam affirms that God is different from any creature. God and creature are radically other. Specifically in relation to the power of God, Islam affirms that God's sovereignty has no competitor. More than this, the power of God in Islam is different in quality as well as in magnitude. As I noted earlier, the Qur'an teaches that Allah is not only all-powerful but also compassionate and merciful beyond comparison with any creature. Among the ninety-nine names of Allah, he is called "the Compassionate," "the Merciful," "the Benevolent," "the Generous," "the Gentle," "the Forgiver" (the last some 125 times in the Qur'an).[16]

Despite its multiple ascriptions to Allah of care, generosity, kindness, and forgiveness, however, the Islamic understanding of God does not include God's personal participation in the human condition even to suffering and death on our behalf. It is here that the difference between the Muslim and the Christian understandings of God and God's power is most apparent.

While rejecting the deity of Jesus Christ, the Qur'an and Muslim theologians speak respectfully of Jesus.[17] He is held in high regard as one of the great prophets of Allah, second only to Muhammad. His virgin birth is acknowledged (3:47), as are his miracles (5:110), his being strengthened with the Holy Spirit (2:87), and his being raised up to Allah (3:55). Conspicuous by its absence, however, is any recognition by the Qur'an of the crucifixion of Jesus. Some Muslim theologians speculate that Simon of Cyrene or someone else was crucified rather than Jesus. Others hold that Jesus died a natural death and then was raised up by God. The denial of the crucifixion reflects an aversion in Islam to thinking of God, or even of one of his great prophets, as experiencing the shameful suffering, humiliation, and death depicted in the biblical passion narratives. Lesslie Newbigin rightly calls this one of the most important differences between Islam and Christianity: "For Islam it is impossible that the cause of Allah should be humiliated and defeated. That is why Muslims, who venerate Jesus, must deny his crucifixion. It would be an inconceivable humiliation of Allah."[18]

While Islam upholds the doctrine that all things are possible to God except what is self-contradictory, the incarnational possibility—the possibility that God's power could take the form of suffering love, could include the capacity to be humble and weak without loss of divinity—is rejected. The Christian doctrines of the incarnation of God's Word, the full deity and humanity of Christ, the atoning death of Christ on the cross, and the Trinitarian nature of God are in the final analysis all about this outrageous possibility. They are all about the embodied, costly grace of God given to us abundantly and beyond all that we deserve. They are efforts to affirm the sole lordship of God who freely chooses a servant form to communicate God's self-giving love to the world not only in word and from a distance but also in deed and up close. In the encounter of Islam and the Christian gospel Christians may become more acutely aware of the difference between speaking of the compassionate God and speaking of "the crucified God."[19]

The Christian understanding of God's exercise of power in the weakness of the cross provides a distinctive Christian basis for the recognition of religious freedom. The principle of religious freedom has been established in democratic societies since the Enlightenment, and no Christian should regret this development or want to reverse it. But the principle of religious freedom does not stand solely on secular grounds. It has a basis also in the Christian understanding of the God of the gospel. Recall the declaration in the third-century *Epistle to Diognetus* quoted earlier: "Compulsion is not God's way of working." Christians are to bear fearless witness to the truth of the gospel in all times and places, but they may not use coercion of any form to enforce this witness.[20] The post-Constantinian church attempted at times to justify compulsion in matters of faith. Those attempts were serious departures from the witness of the New Testament to the crucified Lord.

If I now offer some further reflections on the doctrine of the Trinity, I do so not as an argument directed at Islam, but as an exercise of faith seeking understanding, as an indispensable task of the church in a time of new encounters with Islam. Since I have already discussed some aspects of Trinitarian doctrine in previous chapters, my comments will be largely a reiteration of what I said there.[21] One essential point is that this doctrine is not the product of abstract speculation or the conclusion of an argument from reason alone. The doctrine of the Trinity—that the one God is Father, Son, and Holy Spirit, "one in essence, distinct in three persons"—is a confession of faith. It is all about the surprising and extravagant gift of God's grace.

In saying that the doctrine of the Trinity is a confession of faith, I mean that it is a summary of the gospel of God attested in Scripture, proclaimed in Christian worship, and witnessed in Christian life and service. I mean that for Christians the one and only God who calls for our unconditional trust and praise is decisively revealed in the self-giving love of the crucified and risen Jesus, in the love of the Father who sent him, and in the life-giving Spirit who pours God's love into our hearts. Properly understood, the doctrine of the Trinity has everything to do with the scandal of the cross and the indelible mark it makes on our understanding of God. As a summary of the gospel, the doctrine of the Trinity affirms that God is one with the eternal Logos of God incarnate in the crucified Jesus, and one with his life-giving Spirit.

As enshrined in Trinity doctrine, the otherness of the one God, as confessed by Christian faith, can be stated in several ways. First,

Trinitarian doctrine describes God's power as altogether different from our finite and sinful human experience and exercise of power. God's power is communicative power, shared power, both in God's own eternal life and in God's relationship to the world. The power of God is different from the mere power to transcend the world and exercise absolute control over the world. God's transcendent power is greater still.[22] God is not the prisoner of his transcendence. God is more than free *from* the world; God freely chooses to be *for* the world. Just as God's different transcendence includes the capacity to be immanent without ceasing to be transcendent, so God's different power includes the possibility to be dependent and weak, yet without ceasing to be truly God. To say that God has the capacity to be weak is not to say that God is impotent. On the contrary, it is to say that the cross manifests God's strength in weakness even as it manifests the weakness of the supposed strength of the powers of this world.

This is the theme of the apostle Paul's proclamation of the "weakness of God" that is manifest by the cross (1 Cor. 1:25). What Gentiles find weak, ineffective, and pitiable is the very power of God for salvation. What is considered power by a faithless world—the ability to control and dominate others, the capacity to have one's way regardless of the harm that it does to others   is at the end of the day a display of weakness. God's power in weakness is shown in God's freedom to humble himself, to accept vulnerability, to give himself for the good of others, to exercise patience, and to reject coercion as the means of accomplishing the divine purposes. God in Jesus Christ does for us sinners, prone ever and again to abuse our power, what we cannot do for ourselves. God's love and forgiveness embodied in Christ is sheer gift. In acting for us as one of us, God does not forfeit or abridge his deity but precisely thereby manifests the true difference of his power. Trinity doctrine affirms that this power of God to be God in loving relationship, in life with and for another, belongs to the eternal being of God.

Second and closely related, Trinity doctrine affirms that the unity of God is a union of communion. Does a proper understanding of God as Trinity compromise God's oneness and veer off into polytheism? The confession that God and God alone is Lord is the unbreakable bond between Islam, Judaism, and Christianity. The divergence comes at the point of understanding the unity of God. The oneness of

God, says Trinity doctrine, is not a state but an event. The unity of God is a living, dynamic, eventful unity. The unity of God is greater than sheer oneness. It is deeper than undifferentiated singleness. The unity of the triune God is in communion, in the sharing of love. The communion that is God's life is one in which "no one is out to assert power over others."[23] In technical Trinitarian language, the unity of God is "perichoretic" unity, the mutual indwelling and mutual self-giving love of Father, Son, and Holy Spirit. According to Trinity doctrine, the one God freely loves in God's own being in all eternity and freely shares that love with us, drawing us into communion with God and one another. The chief end of our human existence is to take part in the triune love of God extended to us by Jesus Christ in the power of the Holy Spirit.

Third, the doctrine of the Trinity affirms the reality of personal distinctions in the one act of life in mutual love that is God. According to the doctrine of the Trinity, communion in love is ultimate, but so also are the distinctions of persons in communion. Personal distinctions are of lasting significance; they belong to what is ultimately real. The differences of persons in relationship are of abiding worth. While holding fiercely to the oneness of God, the doctrine of the Trinity also affirms, as a deep ontological truth, the primordial reality of difference in personal relationships. There is, to borrow a phrase from Rabbi Jonathan Sachs, a "dignity of difference."[24] According to the doctrine of the Trinity, this dignity of personal difference goes to the depths of reality. As William Placher puts it, "One of the central insights provided by the doctrine of the Trinity is that *difference is all right*."[25] Islam surely agrees that God affirms difference in creating a world other than God and in creating the plenitude of differences among his creatures. But the doctrine of the Trinity goes one step further and affirms that God's own life includes otherness; it includes abiding distinctions of persons in relationship.

Thus Christians and Muslims have profound agreements and disagreements. They agree that God is other, "Wholly Other" to use the language of the early Barth. They also agree that making God in our own image is idolatrous and destructive. Where Christianity and Islam most profoundly disagree is whether God's love takes the costly form of incarnation and crucifixion. They profoundly disagree whether God freely loves not only in relation to the world but in God's own life. They profoundly disagree whether the reality of the one and only God makes room for difference, not only among the creatures but in God's own being. For Christian faith, the communion of Father, Son, and Holy Spirit is an eternal actuality. This union of communion belongs to the very reality of God in whom distinctions of persons in relationship is not divisive but the fullness of life.

Confessing God as triune raises, of course, the important practical question of whether the Christian community bears credible witness to a form of life in which differences among persons in relationship enhance rather than divide. Is the Christian community one in which identity is not threatened by difference but one in which different gifts are celebrated as having their source in a God who is eternally rich? Is the mutual gift giving of persons in community the meaning of existence in the image of God because it points, however partially and brokenly, to the unique life of God in the mutually shared love of Father, Son, and Holy Spirit? Christian identity in the image of the triune God is not closed but "open identity," open to the other.[26] Might this way of understanding human identity as open rather than closed to others take on new significance in the encounter between Christianity and Islam?

The triune God is the one and only Lord, but this one and only Lord exists not in solitariness but in the communion of self-giving love of Father, Son, and Holy Spirit. God freely loves us from all eternity because in all eternity God *is* love. The power of the one God is indeed *different*. It is the power of "self-sharing for the good of others."[27]

## Conclusion

In the brief span of this chapter I could take only a few steps in the direction of a new theological conversation between Christianity and Islam in our time. My primary focus has been theological, and even here I have only scratched the surface. I have hardly touched on many important practical issues in the Christian-Muslim encounter today, such as universal human rights, freedom of speech, respect for different religious communities, and especially the rights of women. These are topics that are bound to arise in any dialogue between Christians and Muslims today. While Christians naturally hope for the strengthening of reform movements in Islam that are attempting to show there is a basis in Islam's own scriptural sources for open, pluralistic societies dedicated to justice, peace, and the equality of persons, it is important to realize that the Christian church, as it engages in new encounters with Islam, is itself called to be open once again to reform by the living Word of God.

I conclude with three summary affirmations regarding the importance of fostering a new spirit in the meeting of Christianity and Islam.

First, Christians are called to relate to Muslims in the confidence that the grace of God made known in Jesus Christ is at work by the power of God's Spirit even where it is not recognized as present. Such an affirmation requires an openness to the working of the Word and Spirit of God beyond the boundaries of the church. To be sure, the living Word of God addresses us by the power of the Spirit through the proclamation of the gospel and the celebration of the sacraments. But the living Word also addresses us in the presence and the voice of the other and the stranger. The question is whether we have ears to hear, and whether, when appropriate, we show a readiness to repent. In the encounter with people of other faiths, and most especially in our time with Muslims, Christians must be willing to listen as well as speak, must be open to receive fresh insight and deeper understanding of another's faith, and even of their own faith from a very unexpected source. According to the prophet's vision of the new Jerusalem, people will bring into it "the glory and the honor of the nations" (Rev. 21:26).

Second, the interaction of Christians and Muslims requires genuine openness, yet without relinquishing the responsibility to communicate the gospel as faithfully and as persuasively as possible. Fruitful encounter between Christians and Muslims occurs when each faith tradition speaks with clarity and honesty out of the central logic of its faith. Christians should speak and act in this encounter as committed and unashamed Christians, not pretending to be otherwise, and not seeking the presumed safety and detached objectivity of mere observers. I have no doubt that Muslims will want to do the same. A real danger lurks in the call to openness in dialogue with other religions, especially when it is undertaken by those who have largely forgotten or become alienated from their own faith tradition.[28] In dialogue with Islam, Christians will not sweep their central doctrines under the rug even as Muslims will assuredly refuse to hide theirs. The precise outcome of this dialogue cannot be predicted in advance.

Third and finally, the interaction of Christians and Muslims should be encouraged at the grassroots level and fostered in cooperative efforts on matters of common concern and commitment. Even where there are insuperable impasses on doctrinal matters, cooperation in relation to such issues as peace among the nations, justice for all people, food for the hungry, respect for human rights, and protection of the environment from human abuse may be possible. Christians will want to cultivate these possibilities.

## Questions for Discussion

1. How do the ways believers read their sacred books bear on the question whether religion contributes to violence in human life?
2. What are the implications of either affirming or denying that the confession of God alone as the Lord is "the unbreakable bond between Islam, Judaism, and Christianity"?
3. In its encounter with Islam today, should the church focus on proclamation of the gospel or on cooperation in matters of justice and peace? How are the two related?

# Notes

## Chapter 1: The Question of God's Power

1. In analyzing the subject of power, Hannah Arendt distinguishes between the "strength" of persons, the "power" of nations, and the "forces" of nature. While suggestive, I do not think these distinctions can be applied in a mechanical manner. See Hannah Arendt, *On Violence* (New York: Harcourt, Brace, 1970), 56.
2. Walter Wink, *The Powers That Be: Theology for a New Millennium* (New York: Doubleday, 1998), 31. My analysis of the "principalities and powers" is indebted to the work of Wink.
3. Stephen Sykes, *Power and Christian Theology* (London: Continuum, 2006), 152.
4. Paul Tillich, *Systematic Theology*, vol. 1 (Chicago: University of Chicago Press, 1951), 11–14.
5. Martin Luther, *Luther's Large Catechism* (Philadelphia: Augsburg, 1935), 44.
6. Flannery O'Connor, "The Lame Shall Enter First," in *Everything That Rises Must Converge* (New York: Farrar, Straus & Giroux, 1965), 143–90.

## Chapter 2: Images of God's Power in American Culture

1. John Calvin, *Institutes of the Christian Religion*, ed. John T. McNeill, trans. Ford Lewis Battles, 2 vols. (Philadelphia: Westminster, 1960), 1.1.1.
2. Sherwood Anderson, *Winesburg, Ohio: A Group of Tales of Ohio Small-Town Life* (New York: Viking, 1958), 55–109.
3. Colin E. Gunton, *The Actuality of Atonement* (Grand Rapids: Eerdmans, 1989), 51.
4. Calvin, *Institutes*, 1.11.8.
5. John Shelton Lawrence and Robert Jewett, *The Myth of the American Superhero* (Grand Rapids: Eerdmans, 2002), 6–7.

6. Mark I. Pinsky, *The Gospel according to The Simpsons* (Louisville: Westminster John Knox, 2001), 28.
7. Lawrence and Jewett, *Myth of the American Superhero*, 7.
8. Charles Hartshorne, *Omnipotence and Other Theological Mistakes* (Albany: State University of New York, 1984).
9. Robert L. Short, *The Gospel according to Peanuts* (Louisville: Westminster John Knox, 2000), 70.
10. Mark Twain, *The Adventures of Huckleberry Finn* (New York: Bantam, 1965), 12.
11. Jürgen Moltmann, "Introduction," in Ernst Bloch, *Man on His Own: Essays in the Philosophy of Religion* (New York: Herder & Herder, 1970), 28.
12. See N. T. Wright, *The Resurrection of the Son of God* (Minneapolis: Fortress, 2003), 225.
13. Sigmund Freud, *The Future of an Illusion*, trans. W. D. Robson-Scott (New York: Liveright, 1953); *Marx on Religion*, ed. John Raines (Philadelphia: Temple University Press, 2002); Friedrich Nietzsche, *The Anti-Christ, Ecce Homo, Twilight of the Gods and Other Writings*, ed. Aaron Ridley (Cambridge: Cambridge University Press, 2005); Richard Dawkins, *The God Delusion* (New York: Houghton Mifflin, 2006).
14. Paul L. Lehmann, *Ethics in a Christian Context* (New York: Harper & Row, 1963), 112.

## Chapter 3: The Biblical Witness to God's Power

1. Hans Frei, *The Eclipse of Biblical Narrative* (New Haven: Yale University Press, 1974).
2. Hal Lindsey, *The Late Great Planet Earth* (Grand Rapids: Zondervan, 1970); Tim F. LaHaye and Jerry B. Jenkins, *Left Behind: A Novel of the Earth's Last Days* (Tyndale House, 1995). Left Behind is now a multivolume series.
3. Dan Brown, *The Da Vinci Code* (New York: Doubleday, 2003).
4. Karl Barth, "The Strange New World within the Bible," in *The Word of God and the Word of Man*, trans. Douglas Horton (repr. Gloucester, MA: Peter Smith, 1978), 28–50.
5. Terrence E. Fretheim, *The Suffering of God: An Old Testament Perspective* (Philadelphia: Fortress, 1984).
6. See Phyllis Trible, *Texts of Terror: Literary-Feminist Readings of Biblical Narratives* (Philadelphia: Fortress, 1984).
7. George Knight, *Psalms,* vol. 2, Daily Study Bible (Philadelphia: Westminster, 1983), 314.
8. For an excellent discussion of the issues posed by the "psalms of divine wrath," see Erich Zenger, *A God of Vengeance? Understanding the Psalms of Divine Wrath*, trans. Linda Maloney (Louisville: Westminster John Knox, 1996).

9.  Pär Lagerkvist, *Barabbas*, trans. Alan Blair (New York: Random House, 1951), 122.

## Chapter 4: The Power of God in the Theology and Life of the Church

1.  Blaise Pascal, "Pascal's Memorial," in *Great Shorter Works of Pascal*, trans. Emile Caillet and John C. Blankenagel (Philadelphia: Westminster, 1948), 117.
2.  See Martin Hengel, *Christ and Power*, trans. Everett R. Kalin (Philadelphia: Fortress, 1977), 23.
3.  "Letter to Diognetus," in *Early Christian Fathers*, ed. Cyril C. Richardson, Library of Christian Classics (Philadelphia: Westminster, 1953), 219 (7.3 4).
4.  For a brief description of scholasticism in Reformed theology, see Arvin Vos, "Scholasticism," in *Encyclopedia of the Reformed Faith*, ed. Donald K. McKim (Louisville: Westminster John Knox, 1992), 342.
5.  Karl Barth, *Dogmatics in Outline*, trans. G. T. Thompson (New York: Harper Torchbooks, 1959), 48.
6.  Lesslie Newbigin, *Foolishness to the Greeks: The Gospel and Western Culture* (Grand Rapids: Eerdmans, 1986), 101.
7.  Stephen Sykes, *Power and Christian Theology* (London: Continuum, 2006).
8.  Jürgen Moltmann, *The Trinity and the Kingdom: The Doctrine of God*, trans. Margaret Kohl (San Francisco: Harper & Row, 1981), 202; John Yoder, *Body Politics: Five Practices of the Christian Community before a Watching World* (Nashville: Discipleship Resources, 1992).
9.  Karl Barth, *Church Dogmatics*, IV/2, trans. G. W. Bromiley (Edinburgh: T. & T. Clark, 1958), 721.
10. Sykes, *Power and Christian Theology*, 141.
11. Martin Luther King Jr., "Where Do We Go from Here," in *I Have a Dream: Writings and Speeches That Changed the World*, ed. James Melvin Washington (San Francisco: HarperSanFrancisco, 1992), 172.
12. Karl Barth, *Church Dogmatics*, IV/1, trans. G. W. Bromiley (Edinburgh: T. & T. Clark, 1956), 186.

## Chapter 5: The Power of God Who Freely Loves

1.  For two recent introductions to the doctrine of the Trinity, see Philip W. Butin, *The Trinity* (Louisville: Geneva Press, 2001); and William C. Placher, *The Triune God: An Essay in Postliberal Theology* (Louisville: Westminster John Knox, 2007).
2.  For a fuller development of the following paragraphs, see my *Faith Seeking Understanding*, 2nd ed. (Grand Rapids: Eerdmans, 2004), 64–91.

3. William Styron, *Sophie's Choice* (New York: Random House, 1979).
4. Toni Morrison, *The Beloved* (New York: Penguin, 1987).
5. Archibald MacLeish, *J.B.: A Play in Verse* (New York: Houghton Mifflin, 1958), 14.
6. Dietrich Bonhoeffer, *Letters and Papers from Prison*, ed. Eberhard Bethge, enlarged ed. (New York: Macmillan, 1971), 361.
7. See Jürgen Moltmann, *The Way of Jesus Christ: Christology in Messianic Dimensions*, trans. Margaret Kohl (San Francisco: HarperCollins, 1990), 178–79.
8. Alexander Solzhenitsyn, *The Gulag Archipelago*, trans. Thomas P. Whitney, 3 vols. (New York: Harper & Row, 1974).

## Chapter 6: The Reshaping of Power in Christian Life

1. Stephen Sykes, *Power and Christian Theology* (London: Continuum, 2006), 141.
2. For a fine study of the practice of forgiveness, see L. Gregory Jones, *Embodying Forgiveness: A Theological Analysis* (Grand Rapids: Eerdmans, 1995).
3. Miroslav Volf provides moving accounts of what is involved in the acts of reconciliation and forgiveness in two outstanding books: *Exclusion and Embrace: A Theological Exploration of Identity, Otherness, and Reconciliation* (Nashville: Abingdon, 1996); and *Free of Charge: Giving and Forgiving in a Culture Stripped of Grace* (Grand Rapids: Zondervan, 2005).
4. Desmond Tutu, *No Future without Forgiveness* (New York: Doubleday, 1999), 149.
5. Arthur McGill, *Suffering: A Test of Theological Method* (Philadelphia: Westminster, 1982), 99–111.
6. Philip P. Hallie, *Lest Innocent Blood Be Shed: The Story of the Village of Le Chambon, and How Goodness Happened There* (New York: Harper & Row, 1979).
7. Jean-Paul Sartre, *No Exit and Three Other Plays*, trans. L. Abel (New York: Vintage Books, 1955).
8. Martin Luther King Jr., *I Have a Dream: Writings and Speeches That Changed the World*, ed. James Melvin Washington (San Francisco: HarperSanFrancisco, 1992).

## Chapter 7: Toward a Christian-Muslim Dialogue
## on the Power of God

1. For general introductions, see Annemarie Schimmel, *Islam: An Introduction* (Albany: State University of New York Press, 1992); John L. Esposito, *The Straight Path,* 3rd ed. (New York: Oxford University Press, 1998). For detailed studies, see Jane Dammen McAuliffe, ed.,

*Encyclopedia of the Qur'an*, 5 vols. (Leiden: Brill, 2001–2006); Jane Dammen McAuliffe, ed., *The Cambridge Companion to the Qur'an* (New York: Cambridge University Press, 2006).

2.  Quotations from the Qur'an are from the translation by M. A. S. Abdad Harleem, *The Qur'an: A New Translation* (New York: Oxford University Press, 2004).

3.  Fazlur Rahman, *Major Themes of the Qur'ān* (Chicago: Bibliotheca Islamica, 1980), 15.

4.  D. M. Baillie, *God Was in Christ: An Essay on Incarnation and Atonement* (New York: Charles Scribner's Sons, 1948), 114–18.

5.  See Yvonne Sherwood, "Binding–Unbinding: Divided Responses of Judaism, Christianity, and Islam to the 'Sacrifice' of Abraham's Beloved Son," *Journal of the American Academy of Religion* 72:4 (2004): 842.

6.  Bin Laden's letter is reprinted in *The Rise of Islamic Fundamentalism*, ed. Phillip Margulies (Detroit: Greenhaven, 2006), 197–99.

7.  Abdullahi Ahmed An-na'im, *Toward an Islamic Reformation: Civil Liberties, Human Rights, and International Law* (Syracuse: Syracuse University Press, 1990), 144–49. David Cook, *Understanding Jihad* (Berkeley: University of California Press, 2005), argues that Western liberal scholars of Islam tend to downplay the militant meaning of jihad and emphasize instead its spiritual meaning.

8.  See Tariq Ramadan, *Western Muslims and the Future of Islam* (New York: Oxford University Press, 2004); idem, *In the Footsteps of the Prophet: Lessons from the Life of Muhammad* (New York: Oxford University Press, 2006).

9.  See Abdulaziz Sachedina, *The Islamic Roots of Democratic Pluralism* (New York: Oxford University Press, 2001); Khaled Abou El Fadl et al., *Islam and the Challenge of Democracy* (Princeton: Princeton University Press, 2004).

10.  Nicholas Lash, *Believing Three Ways in One God: A Reading of the Apostles' Creed* (Notre Dame: University of Notre Dame Press, 1993), 8.

11.  Karl Barth, *Church Dogmatics*, IV/1, trans. G. W. Bromiley (Edinburgh: T. & T. Clark, 1956), 368.

12.  For an account of an interfaith conversation of a lay group, see Ranya Idliby, Suzanne Oliver, and Priscilla Warner, *The Faith Club: A Muslim, a Christian, a Jew—Three Women Search for Understanding* (New York: Free Press, 2006). For articles by Jewish, Muslim, and Christian scholars involved in a "Scriptural Reasoning Project," see *Modern Theology* 22, no. 3 (2006). A similar Scriptural Reasoning Group of Jews, Muslims, and Christians meets at the Center of Theological Inquiry in Princeton, N.J.

13.  *The Documents of Vatican II*, ed. Walter M. Abbott, S.J. (New York: Guild, 1966), 663.

14. Mark N. Swanson, "The Trinity in Christian-Muslim Conversation," *Dialog* 44, no. 3 (2005): 257.
15. H. Richard Niebuhr, "The Relation of Christianity and Democracy," in *Theology, History, and Culture: Major Unpublished Writings*, ed. William Stacy Johnson (New Haven: Yale University Press, 1996), 148.
16. Rahman, *Major Themes of the Qur'an*, 6.
17. See Tarif Khalidi, *The Muslim Jesus* (Cambridge: Harvard University Press, 2001).
18. Lesslie Newbigin, *Faith and Power* (London: SPCK, 1998), 149.
19. See Jürgen Moltmann, *The Crucified God: The Cross of Christ as the Foundation and Criticism of Christian Theology*, trans. R. A. Wilson and John Bowden (New York: Harper & Row, 1974).
20. Newbigin, *Faith and Power*, 148.
21. See also the chapter on the Trinity in my *Faith Seeking Understanding*, 2nd ed. (Grand Rapids: Eerdmans, 2004), 64–91.
22. Cf. Barth's discussion of the freedom of God in *Church Dogmatics*, II/1, trans. T. H. L. Parker et al. (Edinburgh: T. & T. Clark, 1957).
23. William C. Placher, *The Triune God* (Louisville: Westminster John Knox, 2007), 150.
24. Jonathan Sachs, *The Dignity of Difference: How to Avoid the Clash of Civilizations* (New York: Continuum, 2002).
25. Placher, *Triune God*, 151.
26. Kathryn Tanner, *Economy of Grace* (Minneapolis: Fortress, 2005), 85.
27. See Ian A. McFarland, *Difference and Identity: A Theological Anthropology* (Cleveland: Pilgrim, 2001).
28. John Cobb makes this point in his essay, "The Religions," in *Christian Theology*, ed. Peter C. Hodgson and Robert H. King (Minneapolis: Fortress, 1985), 373.

# For Further Reading

Hannah Arendt, *On Violence*. New York: Harcourt, Brace, 1970.

Karl Barth, "The Strange New World within the Bible." Pp. 28–50 in *The Word of God and the Word of Man*. Translated by Douglas Horton. Repr. Gloucester, MA: Peter Smith, 1978.

Kelton Cobb, *The Blackwell Guide to Theology and Popular Culture*. Malden, Ma.: Blackwell, 2005.

John L. Esposito, *What Everyone Needs to Know about Islam*. New York: Oxford University Press, 2002.

John Kenneth Galbraith, *The Anatomy of Power*. Boston: Houghton Mifflin, 1983.

Daniel L. Migliore, *Faith Seeking Understanding: An Introduction to Christian Theology*. 2nd ed. Grand Rapids: Eerdmans, 2004.

William C. Placher, *The Triune God. An Essay in Postliberal Theology*. Louisville: Westminster John Knox, 2007.

Stephen Sykes, *Power and Christian Theology*. London: Continuum, 2006.

Miroslav Volf, *Free of Charge: Giving and Forgiving in a Culture Stripped of Grace*. Grand Rapids: Zondervan, 2005.

Walter Wink, *The Powers That Be: Theology for a New Millennium*. New York: Doubleday, 1998.